THE WOMAN IN THE WELL

THE WOMAN IN THE WELL

a true story

BARBARA HETTWER

Barbara Lynn Hettwer

Contents

Dedication   viii

1. Fire — 1
2. Ice — 11
3. Well, That Was Unexpected! — 15
4. Rescue — 24
5. Hubert's Story — 29
6. Pete's Story — 34
7. Phil's Story — 45
8. Hospital — 49
9. Jeana's Story — 60
10. Recovery — 64
11. Thoughts To Ponder — 68
12. Preparation — 70
13. Lessons I Learned Well & FAQ — 74

Epilogue	77
Author's Notes	81

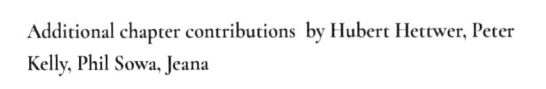

Additional chapter contributions by Hubert Hettwer, Peter Kelly, Phil Sowa, Jeana

Cover photo by Rod Stevens of Stevens Media

Cover Location: Historical Henrietta Saalfeld house wishing well, City of Mt. Angel, Oregon

Inside drawing by Sadie Rose Wuertz

Some photos courtesy of Mt. Angel Fire Department

Copyright © 2024 by Barbara Hettwer

All rights reserved. No part of this book may be reproduced or transmitted in any form or by any means, graphic, electronic, or mechanical, including photocopying, recording, taping, or by any information storage retrieval system, without the written permission of the publisher except in the case of brief quotations embodied in critical articles and reviews.

First Printing, 2024

ISBN 979-8-9904615-0-5

*In Loving Memory
of my brother, Robert W. Bodkin, II*

*Because he clings to me in love, I will deliver him;
I will protect him, because he knows my name.
When he calls to me, I will answer him;
I will be with him in trouble,
I will rescue him and honor him.
With long life I will satisfy him,
and show him my salvation. Psalm 91:14-16*

Recited by my friend, Judy Gabriel, during Aquacize,
August 12, 2021:
*There was an old woman who fell in a well.
I don't know why she fell in a well.
Perhaps she'll tell.*

1

Fire

Early September 2020

Hubert slipped on his shoes and casually stepped into the garage from our home—his normal morning routine to feed our yellow lab, Molly. He soon burst back in, "There's an orange glow over the hills to the east!"

I followed him through the garage and outside into the front yard. Looking past the old hand-dug well and the flowering plum tree, the eastern sky looked like a golden sunrise, but the sun had been up for an hour already.

Hubert opined, "Must be from the Opal Creek fire. They should've put it out when it was only ten acres. Now it's spreading. Well, it's a two hour drive from here. Won't make us no nevermind. Anyway, we don't have any brush that could burn around our house."

As a 26-year volunteer with the Scotts Mills Fire Department, Crooked Finger Station, Hubert knew better than to have big bushes close to our home. My amazing husband had built the house forty years earlier with the help of friend and a stone mason.

The Oregon Cascades form a north-south division between the lush Willamette Valley and arid central Oregon. There are several parallel valleys with rivers or streams flowing westward to the fertile farms. These valleys are separated by high ridges, green with Douglas Fir trees. Our home sat on a ridge top in the foothills at an elevation of 1,850 feet.

We watched the weather report daily. Tension grew as I discovered that Opal Creek was only 23 miles from our home as the crow flies. By September 8, an arid wind of 50 to 75 mph was expected from the east—an extreme wind event unlike anything Oregon had ever seen.

"Hubert, you've lived here all your life. Are they exaggerating?" Being from Southern California, I was not used to extreme weather.

"Well, wind speeds usually aren't that high in the summer. With several fires joining up, it could get bad."

Gale force winds pushed the fire. The conflagration raced down Santiam Canyon faster than escapees could drive. That canyon is the westward water drainage from Detroit Dam in the Cascades. Embers blew as far as 17 miles sparking new fires. Power poles blew down and transformers exploded. The expected route was through the canyon. We are a few ridges north of the canyon. The fire traveled over hills and mountains and through valleys until it was just one mile from our home.

Portland Gas & Electric shut off power in many windy areas to prevent further fire starts from downed lines. There was no power at our house. Our phone landlines run through a green box about 300 yards from our home. It has battery back-up, but that only lasts a day at most, so for weeks to come we had no landline. There is rarely service on our cell phones due to our remote location. We had no water from our well due to lack of power for the pump. Hubert set up his old generator in the detached garage, gassed it up, and crank-started it. He hooked it to our house and ran it enough to keep the food safe in our two refrigerators and two large freezers.

On the morning of September 8, even the inside of our home was smoky. When we went outside to feed Molly, I covered my nose and mouth with my shirt and squinted my eyes, but still the thick orange smoke made my eyes water and my throat burn. The hot wind blew my hair in my face.

"Hubert, this is bad."

"Yeah, it's close."

When Hubert had the generator running so I could get on the internet through our satellite dish, I checked the National Wildfire Coordinating Group. Our neighborhood was under level 3 evacuation orders, which meant "Get out now."

We pulled our SUV up as close to the garage door as we could but were still fighting the wind as we were loading up to leave. Ross from further up the road pulled into our driveway in his pickup. "Hey, Hubert are you leaving?"

"Yep."

"Can I borrow your water wagon?"

"Sure. You mean you're staying?"

"Yeah, the wife's leaving, but I'm not lettin' my house burn. With no power, I can't even water down the roofs of my house and barn. Your water wagon and my generators may save my place."

Hubert was required to have a water source in order to work in the woods as a logger during fire season. The water tank sat on a little trailer. The two men worked to hook it up to the friend's trailer hitch.

With the help of my cousin, Melody who lived with us, we packed up our SUV with Molly in her kennel and boxes of the family photo albums. We stuffed our car with overnight items and my mom's paintings. Following Hubert in his pickup, Melody and I headed to the Willamette Valley, specifically to

St. John Bosco High School, where I volunteer. My brother, Bob, who lived on a neighboring ridge, joined us there. As the principal welcomed us, we assured her that we would not infect the school with COVID germs. The first night we slept in the library cramped on cushy chairs and a small sofa. The next day the principal brought us an air mattress and warm blankets.

Bob was amazing as usual. Throughout my life he had come to my rescue whether it was a scary dog or a broken down car. Now he was staying at his vacation home in Oregon. California was pretty much shut down due to COVID. He had come from there to Oregon to visit and ended up staying for eight months. Being a very sociable person, the idea of eating all his meals at home alone did not appeal to him. We saw each other several times a week for the meager social life that was available during the pandemic.

Bob helped us by arranging the furniture for better sleeping comfort, pumping up the air mattress and paying for many meals. It was a blessing to have him with us.

In order to keep our cold food from going bad, eighty-year-old Hubert drove forty minutes home every day to refuel the generator and run our refrigerators and freezers. His first day back at the house, Ross stopped by again. Hefting his sturdy body down out of his rig, he greeted Hubert, "The wife's back to stay. Are you?"

"No, I'm just here to refuel my generator and keep the food from goin' bad."

The neighbor lamented, "A fire truck pulled into our driveway today with three firemen from a town seventy miles away. I asked if they were here to help. They said, 'No, we're just turning around. This is the price you pay for living out here in such a beautiful area.' Hubert, no one from the outside is gonna help us. We're on our own."

Every few days, cousin Melody and I would accompany Hubert on his trip home. He would run the refrigeration, then flip that circuit off and turn on the hot water heater. After enough time to heat water, he would turn on the water pump. We then took quick showers.

One day when I came back to the house with Hubert, there was a local young man, Jason, stopping cars about halfway up our hill. We stopped to chat.

"I'm just keepin' out folks who shouldn't be here. There are guys going around startin' fires. Neighbors are patrolling at night, and we have a special sheriff assigned to Scotts Mills. They caught one pickup with four guys with incendiary devices in the back. All four guys had previous police records. So I'm just making sure only locals get up this hill."

Hubert asked, "How's the fire fighting going?"

Jason answered, "Really tough. Some guys from the fire department checked out the fire down in Butte Creek canyon. They said it was fine, but we had been down there on our quads and knew it was raging through the tree tops. Luckily, the local volunteer in charge believed us after we showed him the videos on our phones. He put all the effort in that direction. The problem is that the fire department has strict rules. They work from when they finish their morning meetings at 11:30 until 6:00 pm. And they take lunch from 2:00 to 3:00."

"That's crazy," Hubert intervened, "You can't fight a fire like that. A fire doesn't take a nap. It keeps movin'."

"Yep, that's why we local guys fight all night. My brothers and I go to Salem and sleep for a few hours in our pickups each night. The air is easier to breathe there. While we're gone, my Dad mans the fire lines we built."

I asked, "How do you know what you're doing? You're not trained."

"Common sense. When you cut down trees to create a fire break, green goes on green and black goes on black."

I had to have Hubert explain exactly what that meant. To create a fire break, you cut down a swath of trees. If they are burning, you lay them towards the fire. If they are green, you cut them to fall away from the fire.

"You mean you can cut down those trees and make them fall where you want?"

Jason, who grew up in the woods, didn't honor me with an answer. His look said this was elementary stuff for him.

Three days later we ran into Jason's brother, Rick. "How's it going, Rick?"

"Well, the canopy fire has quit, and it is now an underground fire. We keep a fire break at the edge of the trees. It opens up to acres that were logged and is bare dirt with stumps and briers. We try to keep it from flaring up by digging into those black snake trails and putting dirt on them before the fire reaches a big stump."

"That's crazy, I never heard of an underground fire."

"We also made a fire break up here on the ridge. We had two tractors at each end of our big field. They couldn't see each other through the thick smoke, so they turned on their headlights and drove towards each other plowing a path through the hay fields as a fire break. We then pushed that fire line through several properties, including Harvey's land, even though he's out of town."

"Do you think he'll mind?"

"Nope. No one cares about stuff like that now. Barry is lettin' us get all the water we need out of his pond. Word got out, and last night 60 rednecks showed up in their pickups. They placed themselves right along the fire line at the top of the ridge. They were not gonna let the fire get past them. It's awesome how the neighbors, and folks we don't even know, have come together."

I responded, "That is amazing. I'm from Southern California and folks aren't like that there. They just wouldn't know what to do." I had been in Oregon for 30 years and married to Hubert for 21 years. During that time, I learned that country people are smart, tough, and creative out of necessity. They don't hesitate to help their neighbors in an emergency as official help may be slow in coming.

Rick continued "My sister fell into a burn hole. You know, a tree root burnin'. You can't see it, and she just slipped down in. There was no one around. She pulled her feet out of the hole. Embers were in one of her boots! She quick yanked that boot off, went to her four-wheeler and poured water on her foot. It'll take a while for that to heal up."

~~~~~~~~~~~~~~~~~~~~~~

We continued sleeping at the high school but were careful not to interact with the students due to strict COVID 19 regulations. When students were safely tucked inside their classrooms, I would tiptoe down the hallway to use the restroom—being careful to wash my hands and wipe down surfaces. Molly slept in her crate near the outside corner of the building. Hubert, Melody, Bob, and I dined on two meals a day at nearby restaurants, donning masks and socially distancing from the other patrons.

The fire lasted from August 16 through December 10, although we were only evacuated for a week from September 8 through September 14. The last day at the school, I took a nap. As I drifted off to sleep, I played with my wedding ring, twisting it on my finger. When we got home, my wedding ring was gone. It must have slipped off. The next day, Bob and I searched the library, moving furniture to inspect every tiny corner. Then, the students combed through the library with no luck. I went back with a man with a metal detector who made a thorough search of the school yard, especially where Molly had been tied up or walked on her leash, but the ring was never found. I put in an insurance claim and got a small amount compared to what it was worth. We bought a new tiny ring. Hubert didn't blame me for losing my ring, and I didn't cry about it, although I am still sad.

~~~~~~~~~~~~~~~~~~~~~~

Incident Report: Beachie Creek Fire Update, September 17, 2020

> "The emphasis for Thursday is to protect communities to the south and west of the fire. Firefighters will continue to directly attack the fire around Scotts Mills, Stayton, Lyons, Mill City, and Detroit. Other crews are working to protect timber investments on the north side of the fire near Scotts Mills." *(CentralOregonFire.org)*

In the end three fires merged—Beachie Creek, Santiam, and Lionshead—destroying a total of 313,110 acres, qualifying it as one of the largest blazes in Oregon's history. Sadly, five people died in the Beachie Creek Fire, including a thirteen year old boy and his grandmother. George Atiyeh, an environmentalist who saved Opal Creek from clear-cutters years earlier, had refused to leave his home, thinking he was safe. He also perished.

After the fire and despite Corona virus, we returned to our usual routine: attending our tiny local church, shopping in grocery stores, and visiting with neighbors and relatives who dropped by—although outside instead of indoors since none of us wore masks unless required.

~~~~~~~~~~~~~~~~~~~~~

From August through October, I worked for the 2020 U.S. Census. I enjoyed driving around discovering unknown neighbors and unfamiliar roads. There were new adventures every day. Census workers are not trespassers and can knock on any door. It was tough to breathe the smoky air, and I felt even more suffocated in a mask, yet I dutifully donned one before I knocked on any doors.

At one home, I parked on the grassy side of a curvy road, crawled under a gate marked "No Trespassing", and walked across a bridge with a creek rushing over rocks about twelve feet below. When I reached the center of the bridge, a sign read, "You are no longer a trespasser, you are now a target." That didn't stop me, as it's the kind of sign we might put up. The bridge was new and well built. I figured, *Crazy druggies don't have such nice construction.* I walked past a small shop and a lawn with mower tracks revealing recent care. Beyond that on my right were trees creating a park-like setting. A little further on to my left, there was a small, one-story home on the bluff above the creek. I knocked on the door of a screened-in patio and was greeted by a yipping dog. The door from the house opened and a lady peeked out. She smiled and stepped out. She stayed inside the porch but was very friendly.

I showed my badge, "Hello, I'm Barbara from the U.S. Census Bureau."

"How did you get in here? Was that gate open again? There's something wrong with the power to it, and it just opens on its own sometimes."

"No, it was closed. I crawled under it."

I collected the required information, then commented that they had a lovely place. She shared her story of how they searched for three years until they found the perfect home. They loved living there. By the time I left, I felt as though I had made a new friend.

There were many similarly pleasant encounters. I was only run off two properties with yells and threats.

However, due to the fire, the job became quite unpleasant. Many of the locations that hadn't responded to the mailed census questionnaire nor filled out their information online, were in the fire zone.

One day I was sent to an address in Elkhorn past the Elkhorn Golf Course in the Santiam Canyon. The road was blocked, but there was room to get around the barricade. I pondered briefly. A couple sat in their 4WD vehicle near the barricade. I approached them and asked if I could go through. They told me they had purchased a cabin up there two months earlier and couldn't get to it. Most of the houses were burned, and the road had sinkholes and downed trees. I didn't attempt that drive.

I resorted to phone calls when the Census Bureau was able to get cell phone numbers.

"Hello, is this _____?"

"Yes," a female voice responded.

"My name is Barbara Hettwer. I am calling from the U.S. Census regarding the property at _____"

Hesitation, "Yes?"

"I am sorry. I know the house at that location was probably in the path of the fire. I need to inquire about who lived there on April 1st of this year."

"Uh, yes, my house did burn."

"I am so sorry. Would you be able to speak to me and answer some questions? If this isn't a good time, I can call back."

"This is fine. I am not working. The office where I worked also burned."

I proceeded with my questions. She answered in a soft voice. At the end, I apologized for bothering her, and told her my house was spared, and that I couldn't imagine what it must be like for her. It surprised me that these traumatized people were always willing to talk. In some odd way, it may have comforted them to relate their story and receive sympathy. I kept a tissue nearby and dabbed my eyes during these conversations. Unlike some of my co-workers who were driven to quit at that time, unable to withstand the sorrow, I survived this task without becoming too discouraged or depressed. Life happens.

2

Ice

The endless struggle to keep our old bodies in good physical shape occupied our January. I was 70 and Hubert was 80 years old. We had begun seeing a doctor who focused on natural methods of healing and had us on a difficult lectin-free diet. Hubert had an appointment with his cardiologist and tested out fine—always a relief since his quadruple bypass surgery in 2015.

One morning as I was headed outside into the garage, my left ankle twisted, and I fell off the stairs landing on my back on the concrete floor. My head hit the open man-door. It swung shut. I froze, afraid to move. I waited a few minutes to normalize my breathing. I could still hear the thud inside my head from bumping the door. I slowly rolled onto my side then crawled up the two stairs. I reached up and turned the doorknob. Opening the door a few inches, I called, "Hubert! Hubert! I need help."

He walked around the corner from the kitchen to the entryway. He gently helped me up as he had when I fell off my horse, Charlie, or tripped over briers in the woods. I survived, just as I had survived those other falls, including being thrown from horses seven times. This fall did result in four chiropractor visits in January.

My determination to get in shape was undeterred. My neighbor continued to join me once a week for an hour of exercise. We had started a year earlier, before COVID. Our routine had moved from indoors to outdoors due to the pandemic. It was cold so we wore extra layers of clothing.

The last week in January and first week in February, our nine-year old grandson stayed with us. During that time we took him on a little trip to Baker City in Eastern Oregon in an attempt to buy a newer backhoe with no success. The old backhoe would have to do for a while. Amid all of this activity, I continued to volunteer every Wednesday as a secretary at St. John Bosco High School, go to Mass on Sunday, attend a prayer meeting every Tuesday evening, serve on a school board, and once a month meet with a writer's group.

This was my typical life: abundant.

On February 12, the local meteorologists were predicting a severe ice storm. A rare event was uniting icy winds from the Rockies and rain from the Pacific. The rain would freeze upon hitting the ground. We filled the bathtub with water. That was our water supply for flushing toilets when there was no power. I checked my ten one-gallon jugs of drinking water to be sure they were all full.

On Saturday, February 13, I stepped outside, careful to not fall off the stairs. A blast of cold air stung my face. I stayed in the garage and peered out the man door. There was a glassy glow on the entire world. A quarter inch of ice covered everything: the ground, tree branches, the wooden top of the old well, and the wires running from the street to our woodshed.

The power was out, again.

"I'd better start up the generator," Hubert wisely concluded. "This will be a long one."

Once he had some power running to the house, I turned on the TV. The only story was news about the ice. In the Willamette Valley, things were much worse than in the hills. There was a full inch of ice coating everything. Three hundred thousand homes were without power. Many roads were closed due to the tens of thousands of trees that had come down under the weight of the ice.

I joked, "This is a great year: COVID, fire, ice. Are we having fun yet?"

A few days later, I decided to brave the roads to town to buy groceries. As I headed down Crooked Finger Road, I entered a nightmare. Two miles down our winding road the wires normally crossed over the road. The pole was down on one side but not the other. The wires swooped from the top of one pole to the ground on the other side of the road. I maneuvered my vehicle to the side of the road where the line was highest. There were no orange cones. Folks just drove slower and wove their way through the maze allowing opposing vehicles to negotiate their best path. Neighbors worked along the roadside with their power saws to clear trees and limbs. To get to the grocery store, I drove over six power lines and under five swooping ones. In town there were sometimes as many as six poles in a row that had fallen like dominoes. The line for gas in the little town of Silverton was over a block long and took 45 minutes. The ice had melted but the destruction would take a year to clean up.

Due to the lack of electricity, our landlines were out again. On Wednesday evening, February 17, I turned on my computer during the window of time that Hubert ran the generator. I emailed my daughter-in-law, Steph, who was scheduled to bring her two youngest children to stay with us on Friday. I wanted to tell her that it was fine. We could manage with the three- and five-year-old even though we had no power. Steph was to fly to New York with her ten year old to drive her mother (and her possessions) to the Northwest. The nine year old was to stay home with his Dad—a complicated, but well crafted plan. Thursday morning, I discovered that my email had not gone through.

Hubert was planning a trip to town that day. I made sure I had our lectin-free, keto-friendly breakfast made by 9:15 so he could get an early start. I gobbled down my breakfast and looked at the clock. It was 9:30. "Hubert, my email to Steph didn't go through. I'm taking both our cell phones outside to try for a signal."

The highest point in our front yard was on top of the hundred-year-old hand-dug well. Hubert had measured it once and said it was 54 feet deep with the bottom 14 feet being water. It was about three feet in diameter for the depth of the first thirty feet, then narrowed to rougher sides and a diameter of about 2.5 feet. A two-foot high, seven-foot square concrete wall surrounded it at the top. Hubert had re-covered it with 4 x 12 Douglas fir planks twelve years earlier. I stood on top of that platform, which had provided me with a cell signal in the past. I held a phone in each hand above my head and watched their screens for signal bars. None.

3

Well, That Was Unexpected!

I plummeted straight downward in a dark tunnel. My feet hit water. I shot vertically straight down under the water then bobbed slowly back to the surface. My head rose above the water level with my body still upright. I looked around in the dark and saw only a small opening of light above.

I'm in the well! was the first thought I had after my three second trip into a Star Trekish nightmare.

I put my feet on the wall in front of me and pressed my back against the wall behind me. My feet, shod in old athletic shoes, found a small outcropping of rock, about a foot below the water's surface. It was just big enough to support my toes and about a half inch of the balls of my feet. The narrow well, like a tube, encased me, with my nose almost touching my knees. I attempted to secure myself better and reached with my arms to the walls on either side. My right arm didn't move. I gave no thought as to why. My left hand found a tiny rock to grasp with my fingertips for more stability. Surely, I might die. *God, I'm sorry for all my sins.*

I needed to call for help. I took the deepest breath I could and belted out, "Help!" Then I screeched in my highest pitch, "Aaahhh!" followed by another loud yell, "I'm in the well!" I shouted loud enough to strain my throat.

Drawing by my great niece of me in the well because many friends said they couldn't understand my position.
Sadie Rose Wuertz

Maybe I can climb out. I made an attempt to push against the sides with my hands and raise myself up, but again my right arm didn't move. Using two feet and one arm, I could possibly get ten feet before the sides of the tunnel above me became smooth instead of rough and uneven, then there would be no toeholds. That wouldn't work; I would have to wait immersed in the cold water up to my armpits. Hubert would come out in the next half hour.

For twelve years in Catholic schools, whenever there was a problem, the nuns had said, "Offer it up."

God, I offer up all my suffering for the salvation of my children, grandchildren, and godchildren.

Hubert's car was parked in the front yard. He would come out of the kitchen after he was finished with breakfast. The path to his car would take him right past the well in front of the house.

"Help!" I yelled. "Aaahhh!" I screeched. "I'm in the well."

I just have to hold on until Hubert comes out. Maybe it's only fifteen more minutes. That's okay. I'm secure.

"I shall live and not die," I boldly proclaimed.

"Help!" I yelled. "Aaahhh!" I screeched. "I'm in the well."

I'll keep yelling this same way. The regular yell is in one pitch, and the scream is in a higher pitch. Maybe someone further away or with different hearing ranges will hear me.

I listened. There was no noise from above. I waited, listening more intently. *Maybe someone is coming.* No one came.

I was tired and cold. *God, you have to help me.*

"Help!" I yelled. "Aaahhh!" I screeched. "I'm in the well."

God I'm sorry for being selfish.

I saw my fleece-lined denim jacket floating in the water. *How did it get off me? It must have come off over my head, and the force of hitting the water must have pulled the sleeves from my upraised arms.*

"Help!" I yelled. "Aaahhh!" I screeched. "I'm in the well."

Hubert, where are you? How can it take you so long? I shall live and not die. God, I'm sorry for my sins, especially my selfishness. I offer up my suffering for the salvation of my children, grandchildren, and godchildren.

"Help!" I yelled. "Aaahhh!" I screeched. "I'm in the well."

I knew the water was cold, very cold. I wasn't shivering and didn't feel my body temperature lowering, but it had to be.

I was cold, but my teeth weren't chattering. It was a deep in the bone marrow cold. *I could get hypothermia.* "Hypothermia, you cannot have me in the name of Jesus."

"Hubert! Melody! Molly!" Down so far in the well, Hubert probably wouldn't hear me as the kitchen window was closed. My cousin Melody's bedroom was in the front of the house, but it was at the far end, the furthest bedroom from the well. She wouldn't hear me either.

Too bad Molly, our sweet dog, isn't more like Lassie who always saved her owner on TV. I'd better not call her anymore. If she did come, she might look over the edge of the broken boards and fall in. I would drown if she were splashing around in here with me.

The well smelled cool and fresh. The water seemed like a cool mountain pool, but it was too cold. I grew tired and sleepy. *God, wrap me in the warmth of your love.* I felt my body temperature rise.

"Help!" I yelled. "Aaahhh!" I screeched. "I'm in the well."

Jesus, I join my suffering to that of Yours on the cross.

I was wearing a long-sleeved turtleneck. I noticed the left side was pulled up nearly to my armpit. My stomach was showing. The raised back of my shirt left my bare back against the rough-hewn stone wall. I didn't try to adjust it. My mind was occupied with a more urgent matter—to stay alive until help came.

My throat was dry. I thought I could drink the water to soothe my throat. In my scrunched position, with my torso bent forward, the water was not far from my mouth. Floating before my eyes, were bits of wood, moss, and tiny purple leaves from the plum tree above. *If the water has bacteria, doctors can get rid of that after I'm out of here. I have to be able to keep shouting.* I blew on the water in front of me and the debris floated away. I leaned my head more forward and sucked up some water. It was cool and pure.

"Help!" I yelled. "Aaahhh!" I screeched. "I'm in the well."

God, You can't let me die. Hubert is such a good man, and he would feel so bad if I died. You have to save me.

"Help!" I yelled. "Aaahhh!" I screeched. "I'm in the well."

God, if I get out of here, I will try not to be selfish anymore. I will tell everyone that it is You who saved me.

"Hypothermia, GO! In the Name of Jesus."

"Help!" I yelled. "Aaahhh!" I screeched. "I'm in the well."

What is Hubert doing? How can it take this long?

"Melody! Hubert!"

God, you can't let me die. I prayed the St. Bridget prayers and asked to not die without Viaticum—receiving Holy Communion right before my death. I know I am supposed to pray those prayers every day and I only prayed for a while, but please honor that. There is no priest in this well to give me Holy Communion, so You can't let me die.

"Help!" I yelled. "Aaahhh!" I screeched. "I'm in the well."

My right shoulder throbbed. I leaned to the right just a few inches to dip it in the cold water. It helped. My mind drifted. Thoughts were hard to hold steady.

If it's going to be much longer, I need to keep myself awake. I'll pray the Rosary. That takes about twenty minutes. Hubert will surely come out by then. It will keep me occupied and awake. It's Thursday—that is the Luminous Mysteries.

As a child in Catholic school, I had learned to pray the Rosary, which is a meditative prayer focusing on events in the life of Jesus. My sister and brother, Diane and Bobby, and I used to pray it together at night after we were in bed. Our doors were open so we could hear each other from our different rooms.

Taking as deep a breath as I could, I began, "In the Name of the Father, and of the Son, and of the Holy Spirit, Amen." I softly mouthed the words of the Apostle's Creed, "I believe in God, the Father Almighty, Creator of Heaven and Earth…"

I sipped more water.

"Help!" I yelled. "Aaahhh!" I screeched. "I'm in the well."

I continued the Rosary with an Our Father, three Hail Mary's, and a Glory Be.

What's next? I have to think. The first Luminous Mystery, the Baptism of Jesus in the Jordan River. Oh, this is a new baptism in my life. Here I am in water. God is baptizing me anew for a new purpose.

"Help!" I yelled. "Aaahhh!" I screeched. "I'm in the well."

I said most of the prayers quietly or silently to save my breath and throat.

"Our Father, Who art in Heaven..."

In my mind, I clearly saw the Jordan river, John the Baptist, and Jesus. I was right there observing the event. In 1994, I kayaked on the Jordan River and swam in it. I know how it looks and feels. There in the well, I didn't just remember it, but actually re-experienced being there: the cool rippling water and the willow trees along the banks. For each of the five mysteries, I focused on the specific mystery while reciting the prayers. I kept track of the ten *Hail Mary* prayers on my fingers as I would often do when I prayed the Rosary while swimming. I just put a little pressure on each finger as the count advanced.

I added, "Glory Be to the Father, and to the Son, and to the Holy Spirit..."

Oh, Lord, don't let one of my grandchildren be lost.

"Help!" I yelled. "Aaahhh!" I screeched. "I'm in the well."

I leaned my right shoulder into the cold water again to ease the pain.

Blessed Mother, wrap me in your mantle to keep me warm. The second Luminous Mystery. What is it? Uhhh...Jesus works His first miracle at the wedding feast at Cana. Lord, I pray for all the marriages in our family. I especially pray for Hubert. Save me for his sake. Work a miracle and get me out of here.

"Our Father, Who art in Heaven..."

I was there. I could see the room or cave at Cana where I had been in 1994. I could see the water pitchers and Jesus talking with His mother and the servants. "Hail Mary... (10x), Glory Be... Oh my Jesus..."

"Help!" I yelled "Aaahhh!" I screeched. "I'm in the well."

The third Luminous Mystery, Jesus preaches the Gospel. I could see Jesus on the Mount of Beatitudes in Galilee where I had been in 1988. He was speaking in a clear voice to a multitude sitting on the hillside. I was standing watching the multitude; the sky was a clear blue; Jesus' voice carried to my ears. I prayed, "Our Father... Hail Mary... (10x), Glory Be... Oh my Jesus..."

Lord, if I get out of here, I will share the Gospel message. I will let people know that You saved me because only You can keep me alive at this point.

"Help!" I yelled. "Aaahhh!" I screeched. "I'm in the well."

The fourth Luminous Mystery, The Transfiguration. I was up on Mt. Tabor watching Jesus, glorified with Moses and Elijah. Peter, James, and John were there, awestruck. "Our Father... Hail Mary... (10x), Glory Be... Oh my Jesus..."

"Help!" I yelled. "Aaahhh!" I screeched. "I'm in the well."

The fifth Luminous Mystery, Jesus establishes the Eucharist at the Last Supper. I could imagine the room where this took place. In 1988, I had been in a room in Jerusalem called the Upper Room. It is a large room, the type of room where such a meal could have taken place. I experienced the Apostles sitting around the table. Jesus held up the unleavened bread. There was reverent talking; Jesus said the blessing over the cup. "Our Father... Hail Mary... (10x), Glory Be... Oh my Jesus..."

Oh God, please bring all those who don't believe in the Real Presence of Jesus in the Eucharist to the fullness of the Faith.

"Help!" I yelled. "Aaahhh!" I screeched. "I'm in the well."

I finished the Rosary, and Hubert isn't here! Oh God, how can it take this long?

I dipped my right shoulder in the cool water a third time. I looked at the water before my face. As I exhaled, drifting particles moved away. I sipped deeply to comfort my throat again.

Looking into the water, I wondered what it would feel like to drown. I would only have to remove my feet from the wall in front of me, relax and sink. *No, I don't think that's how I'm going to die.*

It's been so long. "God, how can it take so long? Help me hang on," I groaned.

"Help!" I yelled. "Aaahhh!" I screeched. "I'm in the well."

"Guardian Angel, please go into the house and tell Hubert's guardian angel to prompt him to come out here."

I leaned back and lifted my head, which took effort. In my darkness, the circle of light forty feet above seemed familiar. Thirty-one years earlier, I had seen this light. I was sitting on the couch in the middle of the night after nursing my newborn, Mark. Opening my Bible, I read Psalm 40:1-2. "And I waited, waited for the lord, and he stooped toward me and heard my cry. He drew me out of the pit of destruction, out of the mud of the swamp; He set my feet upon a crag; he made firm my steps." I didn't remember the entire verse, but remembered the vision I had at the time because it had greatly impacted me. That night long ago, on the couch with my eyes closed, I experienced being in a pit. I had looked up and seen the opening and bright light far above. The deep pit and circle of light in my vision were now my reality. At that time it was an emotional pit; it never occurred to me there would be a literal pit in my future. In that vision, I saw Jesus up at the top of the well, reaching his hand down toward me to pull me out. That's all there was to the vision. His hand didn't reach me, but I knew I would be rescued. This memory confirmed to me that God would get me out of the well.

"Jesus, thank you for saving me. Thank you for getting me out of here."

How long have I been in this well? It has to be over an hour.

I was getting colder, and it became more difficult to stay awake.

I spoke firmly, "Hypothermia, you have no right to me. I shall live and not die."

"Help!" I yelled. "Aaahhh!" I screeched. "I'm in the well."

I prayed in tongues. I was glad I had that gift since it took no brain power, just letting the Holy Spirit pray through me.

"Help!" I yelled. "Aaahhh!" I screeched. "I'm in the well."

"Guardian Angel, can't you please go into the house and tell Hubert's guardian angel to prompt him to come out here?"

"Help!" I yelled. "Aaahhh!" I screeched. "I'm in the well."

I heard a noise that could have been the door from the house into the garage closing.

"Help!" I yelled. "Aaahhh!" I screeched. "I'm in the well,"

I leaned my head back and looked up as best I could from my crunched position. I saw a shadow in the window of light above.

"I'm in the well."

"Yes, I see that," Hubert calmly responded.

"You have to get me out of here. I need to get out right now!"

"I'll have to go across the street to get help."

"No, I need you to get me out of here NOW!

"I have to go across the street. Hold on. I'll be right back."

"Okay."

He disappeared.

God, Thank you. I can wait. Keep me strong.

4

Rescue

It must have been ten minutes before Hubert returned. He talked to me. I really can't remember much of the next series of events. I was tired and cold and on the verge of losing consciousness. I later found out that I was in the well for two hours alone.

"Hubert, you have to get me out of here right now!"

A neighbor, Shannon, was up above. She said, "Barbara, It's Shannon. Can you hear me?"

I responded, "Hi, Shannon." People have told me that she talked to me for almost two hours and relayed messages between me and the people above. I only remember her talking three times. She knelt on the edge of the well all that time, not moving, getting drenched by the nearly freezing rain.

Hubert shouted down to me, "Pete, from across the street, is coming down into the well." We had met Pete once, six months earlier, on the day his family moved in. We had taken them some gluten-free, blueberry muffins and had a friendly visit in their front yard. Now, he was being lowered into the well by a rope with a harness around him.

I remember Pete saying. "I'm coming down. I'm almost there." He was on my left side. I relaxed onto his lap and leaned against his chest. I remember the warmth of his chest against mine. At one point, I heard Pete shout, "Two more inches!" I presume we were raised up by the rope to get us a little out of the water. My upper body was now free of the icy water. We were still in the water from our waists down.

Voices from above asked if they could pull us up. Pete said he didn't think he could hold me all that way. The rope was attached to his harness, and there was not another rope to attach to me. I couldn't hold onto anything.

Pete and I had pleasant conversation with each other, but we desperately shouted to the folks above to get us out of there. Pete kept encouraging me. He assured me he had his fingers interlocked behind my back and wouldn't let me go. I think I was asleep much of the time and would wake up when he spoke. I remember him adjusting his grasp around my back a few times. Once he said, "Can you hold on to me?" I put my left hand on his shoulder. He let his grip loose and quickly regrasped.

Pete suggested, "Sing me your favorite song."

My brain was simple at that point. It was hard to grasp any thoughts. I had reverted to the most basic ideas in life. I sang, "Jesus loves me this I know." That's all. No more lines of the song. I didn't have the energy.

Pete said, "I like that song. I remember it from when I was a kid."

I asked him to sing a song. He said he knew a prayer that his girls recited at camp. I don't remember the words, but it was very nice. It rhymed and was all about the beauty of nature.

After some more shouting to and from above, and things

being pelted upon us (helmets, wood chips, metallic blankets), I said to Pete, "We're not here."

Pete's voice sounded a little concerned, "We're not?"

"No, we're on the beach in Hawaii."

He immediately joined my fantasy. "Oh, what would you like to drink?"

"I don't drink."

"Neither do I."

"But I would like a Piña Colada," I added.

"Oh, yeah, they're good."

Pete was with me for almost two hours.

I later spoke with the Mt. Angel Fire Chief who was trained for such rescues. He was going to come down, but he heard Salem Fire Department was coming. It was better to wait for the right rigging and more help. He explained how carefully they removed the wood from the top of the well, one board at a time with several guys lifting together so it wouldn't break and fall into the well.

There was much chatter coming from the circle of light above, then a man's voice said, "I'm Bruce. I'm coming down." He came down holding two black harnesses. He explained he would put the one on Pete first, then the two of them would get one on me. Pete told him my right arm was injured. There was much fidgeting. Pete had to let go of me, but I think I was held between their two bodies. After Pete's harness was secure, they both worked to put on mine. Pete said again to be careful of my right arm.

Bruce said he and I would go up together, and then they would lift up Pete. It took courage to let go of Pete and fling my body against a stranger. We arose.

I remember being on my back on a gurney and loaded into an ambulance. There were two men in there with me. One said, "We have to remove your clothes,"

I said, "Okay."

There was more fidgeting. There were blankets put on me.

I felt a jolt. We were moving and only one man was with me.

I was shaking. The pain was nearly unbearable. My body was shivering so badly that I was bouncing. I noticed the information embroidered on the attendant's jacket.

"Your name is Mark, and you're from Woodburn Ambulance."

"Yes."

"Is this pain normal?"

"Yes, I think it is."

"Why did Woodburn come?"

"We were at Salem hospital after bringing another patient, so they sent us."

Mark did several things which I can't remember. Each time he explained what he was going to do.

I asked, "Do you do this often?" He knew I was referring to my hypothermia.

"Not too often. When we get to to Salem, they will have a special blanket called a Bair Hugger. That will warm you up."

"It hurts so much. Is it supposed to hurt this much?"

"I think that's normal."

The pain was truly terrible. It was worse than having my babies with no medication. The excruciating pain wasn't in one spot but engulfed my entire body. I experienced continuous, uncontrollable, violent shaking.

Shannon keeping her 2 hour vigil

Some of the crowd

Backhoe with rigging

Barbara being hoisted from the well

5

Hubert's Story

Barbara fixed breakfast as usual. She ate quickly then told me she was taking both our phones outside to call Steph, our daughter-in-law. I finished breakfast, downed my pills and cleaned up the dishes.

I was going to town that day and had lots to do to get ready. I began by sorting the paper recycling. I put the newspapers in a grocery bag and the white paper neatly on top of the newspapers, then crammed the recycle box full of cans and cardboard and placed it all near the door.

Next, I got the cooler ready for the food I would buy. I always put ice packs in the cooler. There was one large ice pack that we kept in the center front of the big chest freezer in our pantry. I grabbed it and struggled, pulling and wiggling my hand, but couldn't get it out. It was frozen in place with ice build-up.

I thought, *This is ridiculous!* I knew how to fix the problem. I got my favorite spatula, the big plastic one I use to flip burgers on the grill. I jammed it between the ice and the freezer wall and broke off chunks. The ice pack came free plus all the ice around it. I put it all in the big laundry sink. I went to work on the basket tray that held our frozen berries. It took a while, but I scraped the ice away from that side of the freezer and set the basket free to slide as it should. I ended up with about twenty pounds of ice in the sink. Then I got the cooler ready with its big ice pack and placed it near the door.

It had been a long time since Barbara went outside. I looked out the front window and the back door. I didn't see her and wondered how far she had to go to get a signal. I knew she sometimes talked a long time to Steph so I wasn't worried.

I filled my water bottle, added ice, then refilled the ice tray. With my shopping list buttoned into my shirt pocket, I was all ready to go. I opened the door to the garage and stepped out. I heard Barbara hollering.

I saw there were two boards broken on the top of the well. My stomach felt sick. I knew what had happened. I looked down into the well in the cloudy morning gloom and saw something 40 feet down.

"I'm in the well!" Barbara hollered again.

"I see that."

"Get me out now!"

My mind raced. *I can't get her out by myself. How long has she been in there? I can't call for help. Our landline isn't working and both our cell phones are probably in the well! Ray next door is at work. Maybe someone across the street can get a signal on their cell phone.*

"I can't get you out yet. I'll have to go for help."

I went straight across the street to Gena. She tried several times to dial 9-1-1, but it didn't go through. I went to her next-door neighbor, Pete, and saw him out in his yard.

"Does your cell phone work?"

"Yeah."

"Call 9-1-1. Barbara is in the well."

His wife or daughter called 9-1-1.

I walked back home and told Barbara that we had called 9-1-1.

She yelled, "You have to get me out of here now!"

"It's okay. We'll get you out soon. I have to wait for help."

Gena was there and said, "She shouldn't be alone in there. I'll go down." Gena is in her 80's! Pete soon appeared. "I can rappel down there."

Although Pete is a strong, healthy 50-year-old, I knew that was a bad idea.

"No, how can you hang onto a rope and try to do something with Barbara? I'll lower you down. I'll get my backhoe, but we'll need a rope."

By that time others were showing up. Shannon was kneeling at the edge of the well. "My Dad has a rock climbing harness. I'll have someone bring it."

Pete's wife, Kay, said, "I'll go get our long rope."

I got my trusty, old backhoe and put it next to the well. I raised the bucket on the front of the backhoe as high as it could go without hitting the branches on the old plum tree, which stood right next to the well. I centered the bucket as best I could over the well. Kay brought their rope which had been used for rock climbing but in recent years was used to hold up their hammock while camping. It was plenty long but had a little fraying. We figured it was long enough and would be strong enough if we doubled it.

By that time I had a block with a pulley secured on the bucket. A young, strong neighbor, Allen, had shown up. We fitted the harness from Shannon's father onto Pete and hooked him up. With Allen, me, and Pete's family holding the rope, we lowered Pete down. Sometimes he would say, "Wait a minute," as he positioned himself in the pit. It took about five minutes to get him down to Barbara. Once he was holding her, he would direct us occasionally to pull up a little on the rope. It got their torsos out of the cold water.

Even with the block making the weight less, our arms were weakening. Various neighbors helped hold the rope. Allen was in the front and bore the brunt of the effort. We wanted to tie the rope onto something, but there was nothing except Phil's pickup. He was reluctant. We were "Good Samaritans" with no training, using uncertified equipment, and had no rules binding us. We figured that because he was a volunteer for the Silverton Fire Department that he was bound by protocols. When Allen's bulging muscles were shaking, Phil knew we needed help and moved his pickup so we could tie onto his trailer hitch.

People continued to arrive. First, it was neighbors including the volunteer firefighters, then a Silverton firetruck, and then Mt. Angel. Eventually, there were two ambulances. These fire departments didn't rescue Barbara and Pete. I presumed they weren't trained for that. Silverton Fire Department did block the wheels on my backhoe to make sure it wouldn't move.

The rope attached to the backhoe wasn't in great shape. We knew it couldn't pull two people up, so we just had to wait. They did yell, "Get us out of here!" every fifteen minutes or so. It was hard to explain to them why we couldn't get them out. We had to wait for Salem Fire and Rescue.

It was raining the entire time. Everyone standing outside was wet. There were some neighbors in our garage watching and praying. There were about thirty-five people there in all. I was outside; my head was drenched and so was my coat. A neighbor woman said, "Hubert, you need to put on dry clothes." I went down into the furnace room, took off my coat, and put on my fuzzy-lined denim jacket and my hard hat.

Once I was back outside, Pete asked us to raise him up six inches. We untied the rope from the pickup hitch, pulled, and re-tied.

It must have taken forty-five minutes for Salem to arrive. Then I felt confident because I knew they could handle the rescue, and Pete could hold Barbara until then. Salem had straps with a carabiner which they wrapped around the west side of the backhoe bucket. They wanted to take the boards off the top of the well. I got a splitting maul for them to use. They lowered helmets down into the well first so wood wouldn't hit Barbara or Pete. It was probably half an hour from the time the rescuers arrived until they sent a man down.

They slowly raised up the rescuer and Barbara together. I was finally relieved knowing she was still alive and coming out. They pulled Barbara out on the east side and got her torso over the concrete wall. She was lying on her back on the grass with her feet up on the wall. They pulled her legs down one at a time. She turned onto her side. Two guys with a gurney had to step over knee-high ropes to get to her.

I asked if I could ride in the ambulance with her, but they said I couldn't because of COVID restrictions. They took off down the road. Pete couldn't stand up because his legs were too cold. They put him in the other ambulance. I went in the house and changed into dry clothes then headed to the hospital.

6

Pete's Story

I was in the back of the property with six year old Emma feeding the chickens. I was wearing a very old dirty pair of Carhartt pants and my new work boots. The dogs barked and ran toward the gate at the front of the property, then quit barking.

Emma said, "Who's in the pasture?" as she ran towards the front of the property. I could see someone at the gate but couldn't make him out through the thick fog. Luna was wagging her tail telling me it was someone she knew. As I approached, I saw a tall figure walking towards the house and realized it was Hubert. I trotted up and hollered to him.

"What's going on?"
"Do you have any rope?"
"Yeah, I think I have some rope. How much do you need?"
"Oh, I don't know, maybe fifty, hundred foot."
"I have it either in the barn or the camper."
"Could I borrow your phone?"
"Yeah, who do you need to call?"

"Barbara's got both of our phones."

"Well, who do you need to call?"

"I think I need to call 9-1-1. Barbara's down in the well."

At that point, I knew why he needed the rope.

My wife, Kay, had come to the front door because of the noisy dogs.

I shouted, "Call 9-1-1! Barbara's in the well!"

All our phones work differently at different parts of the property. Kay turned to our girls, Maddy, Kassie, and Jo, and told them to dial 9-1-1.

"Kassie, find the red rope that we used for the hammocks. It's either in the barn or the camper." I knew I had about 90 feet of ½ inch rope.

After the fires, Kay set up a texting tree with neighbors to use in case of emergencies. She sent out a text that Barbara was in the well. One neighbor, who was in Idaho at the time, got the text. She replied, "I have a friend named Allen down the road. I'm going to text him." Allen is ex-military. He was in his pasture with his family. They have no cell reception on their property.

His wife said, "Allen, your phone just chimed."

He looked at the text and said, "I gotta go."

Kay and I walked across the street and saw Barbara down in the well. Hubert said she had been in there for at least an hour.

"Hubert, Kassie's looking for rope. Are you sure you don't have any rope in the shop?"

Hubert surmised, "I might have some in the shop."

We went out to his shop and saw electrical wire. "Do you have any extension cords? Anything?"

Hubert found an old piece of yellow nylon rope. We went to the well and leaned over the edge of the broken boards. I lowered the rope. It was just long enough for Barbara to grab the end.

Hubert hollered, "Can you tie it around your waist?"

Barbara responded, "I can't move my arm."

Hubert suggested, "Can you wrap it around your arm?"

She wrapped it around her wrist. We were holding just the end, so it really wasn't long enough to do any good.

My daughter, Jo, was at the end of the driveway to wave down any ambulance or fire people that might come up Crooked Finger Road from Scotts Mills. Allen traveled the four miles from his home to the Hettwer house in three minutes in his big, old Suburban. Kassie showed up with the rope at the same time Allen arrived. Skip, a neighbor I had never met, arrived.

Barbara wearily said, "I'm gonna let go."

When I first looked down there, Barbara was holding herself up about waist deep. Then it was stomach, then chest, then armpits. Barbara kept saying, "I'm just gonna let go. I can't hold on anymore."

We kept saying "Hold on a little bit longer." She insisted, "I can't."

Hubert and I pleaded, "Just a little bit longer."

I had done rock climbing and rappelling and all that. I couldn't let Barbara give up.

"I'm gonna go down there. I'll just go down there and stabilize things."

Skip said, "I have a harness."

I don't know why he would have one. He's 70-something years old.

"Where do you live?"

Skip pointed across the street and down a few houses, "Right over there."

As it turns out, Gena had gone to his house to get him. When he heard her at his door, he checked the temperature. It was 36°. As it turns out, Skip had been a firefighter for 18 years and had worked with the Forest Service. He had been at three well rescues. Once he was the man who was lowered down.

While Skip was gone, the first volunteer fireman showed up with a winch on the front of his pickup. I thought, *Sweet. That will make it easy.*

He had pulled into the parking spot head first. I asked, "How long is your cable on your winch? Can you turn that around?" No answer. "How long is the cable on your winch?"

He got out of his pickup and said, "Nobody's going down there."

I firmly stated, "Yes, I'm going down there because she's about to let go."

"As long as she's talking, nobody's going down there."

That made no sense. If she stopped talking, it would be too late.

It seemed like Skip was gone for two minutes, and he was back with the harness. He quietly said to his wife, "This is not going to end well."

Allen was a bigger guy than me. He said, "I'll lower you down."

Kay insisted, "Pete, You're not going down there."

Allen assured us, "I got this. I will *not* let go."

I was putting on a harness and tying on a loop when fire trucks arrived.

Kay looked at the firemen, "Why is it you guys are all here, and my husband's going down?"

They were videotaping. Maybe it was a liability issue for them. Maybe they weren't trained in well rescue or steep rescue.

Hubert had brought the backhoe over and had a pulley which was helpful. We doubled the rope to make it stronger and put it over the pulley. Allen, Kay, Maddy, Kassie, Hubert, and two other neighbor girls held the rope. I remember getting four feet from Barbara and hearing everything from up above clear as day, but I had to yell for them to hear me. It was bizarre. I don't know why. Maybe because it was raining, snowing, and windy up above. I clearly heard Allen say, "I don't know if we have enough rope."

I assured them, "I just need a few more feet!" They were literally at the end of the rope. We had cut a bunch of rope when we were camping earlier in the summer, so I wasn't sure how much rope I had.

I said, "I just need a little bit more."

I think they gave me another foot or so. I was three feet from Barbara. I remembered my water rescue training from years earlier and knew she might cling to me. She levitated in a last burst of energy—an adrenaline rush—and sprang up straight out of the water and grabbed me. Luckily, I was mentally ready for it. With both of us on it, the rope stretched, which was perfect. If they had let me down to Barbara, and she had grabbed on to me, we probably would have gone bonk into the water, and they would have had to pull us up.

I hugged her. "I got you."

We were both at water level, "Hold us here." I shouted to above.

I was in an awkward position, trying to get situated, so I had them pull us up a little bit. Kay, Skip, Allen, and I thought to get another rope to put on Barbara and pull us both up. Better yet, send the cable down from the winch on the pickup with a burlap sack, a weight-lifting belt, something wide.

"Send me something down here to work with: a blanket, an old hammock. We'll make a harness." I didn't know the weight limit on our rope. The last thing I wanted was us getting pulled up halfway and the thing snapping and us falling back down together, so we needed another rope for Barbara. We ended up waiting and waiting.

I remember looking up at the fire fighters thinking *What are you guys doing? Let's get out of here.*

Barbara came in and out of consciousness. She had brief moments of panic. "I need to get out of here. I need to get out." She would get restless. She kept saying, "My shoulder, my back."

I would say, "Well, let's just not move right now."

She may have been blacking out. She would just chill. I put her head on my shoulder because I was warm. I'm always warm. I can crawl in an igloo and radiate heat. I was also listening to her breathe, which was reassuring.

It must have been an hour until they said, "We're waiting for Salem Steep Rescue. They're trained in this."

I said, "All we need is another rope and some material. Make a sling from a big feed bag. We can do this."

They were going to remove the wood from the top of the well because they were worried about it falling in on us.

I explained, "The wood that fell in here is already in here. Leave it alone, just pull us up out of here. I came in on this rope without touching the wood. You can pull us out without touching the wood. You don't need to clear the wood." They sent down hard hats for our heads and cleared the rest of the boards from above.

They continued working for an hour..."We need to block the wheels of the backhoe...how about the hydraulics?...Are the hydraulics good?...When is the last time it was serviced?..."

They were chaining everything and blocking, locking and chocking. They wanted to have it ready for the Salem Steep Rescue guys.

"Dude, I just came down here on the pulley from the backhoe. It's obviously decent enough. Pull Barbara up, then pull me up."

At this point, I was down there for an hour. Barbara was down there for three hours, and we were still waiting for Salem. We were told, "They'll be here. They're on their way. We just had contact with them. They just flew into the Salem airport. They'll be here in a half hour."

No way. They can't get here in a half hour from Salem airport. They're an hour out, at best.

It turns out that the two guys who came from Salem Steep Rescue had just gotten off a plane in Salem. They were down in Texas doing training because they had the ice storm down there too. They got back from Texas and jumped in the car and came right here with their gear.

At that point the local firefighters lowered down what I call a pulley block. It's designed for hoisting and rappelling. It was three pulleys instead of just one so one person could pull up two or four depending on how you configure it. They also sent down the end of a nice, big, thick rope. I thought, *Perfect*.

From above they said, "Can you tie onto this?"

I said, "You bet I can." I tied onto that rope. "Now do you have any fabric I can tie to the rope that I came down on to make a sling or harness around Barbara? I can bear hug her, and you can pull us up with the two ropes at the same time."

The red rope was yanked hard. "Let go of the rope."

"No, I need this. Drop me down something so I can make a harness, and you can pull us out. This is ridiculous. It's cold. She needs to get out of here!"

"Let go of the rope. Let go of the rope!"

I was holding onto the red rope and holding on to Barbara. They yanked it out of my hand.

"We're waiting for Salem."

"You guys are ridiculous."

When Salem showed up, boom, boom, boom. They were phenomenal. The first guy was going to come down. I was looking up at him.

"I'm looking at your head and shoulders. There's not room for you down here. I can tell you that right now. Who else do you have?"

The other man peered down in. I could see daylight behind him. "Yeah, you come down."

They tried to bring down this huge backboard. I shouted, "How's that going to work. It's six feet long and would have to be hoisted sideways. It's not six feet in diameter down here. There's no room for that thing. Do you have a sling?"

The Salem rescue guy looked at one of the Silverton Fire guys and said, "Do you have a diaper?"

"Yeah."

That was a triangular, waterproof canvassy thing with three grommets at the points. They put one end up through the legs and bring up the sides like a diaper. And click, click, click. The Silverton Fire guys had the gear all along. So in the end, all they did was send down a triangular piece of fabric. It was a sling which I could have made down there with a piece of canvas or anything and attached to another rope.

"Pete, we're going to bring you up first."

"That makes no sense! She's sitting on top of me. Why would you think it makes sense to bring me up first? And do what? No, put the harness on Barbara, and take Barbara out first."

They did, then brought me up. Of course, at that point I couldn't feel anything from my waist down. I couldn't feel my legs. I couldn't move them. Once I got out of the well, I couldn't stand up. Everybody was alive, the adrenaline rush was over. I figured I could go home and get in our sauna and I'd be fine. The head EMT gal said, "Your wife told me you were going to say, 'No' to a trip to the ER."

"Yeah, I'm not going."

"Your wife told me you were going to say that."

I looked around. Kay stared at me. "I guess I'm going to the ER."

Kay said, "You're an idiot."

I answered, "Yeah, I know. I didn't even think twice."

I'm kind of claustrophobic even though I work in tunnels. I work on boilers. But there wasn't even a thought of not going down. Someone had to go down there that was capable of holding on to Barbara. Skip was an older gentleman. Allen is probably 30 to 50 pounds heavier than me. Hubert's older.

He's wasn't going down. And the volunteer fireman obviously wasn't going down. Who else was going to do it? Barbara had just said, "I'm going to let go."

When they pulled Barbara out, they dropped her on the ground right next to the well—on film. They have the film.

When they got me out, we headed to the ER. My ambulance left first. Barbara's ambulance followed us down the hill. After getting through town, they threw their lights on. We moved over and they came flying by. That was worrisome. "Why'd they do that? Why the sirens?"

I went to the ER. Kassie and Kay came to get me. They brought me granola bars and nuts. I just kept saying, "I want some coffee. I want some coffee—something warm right now."

I lost my favorite belt. I had it for 30 years. I got it in Colorado—fantastic little belt. It was just a cheap little woven belt. I took my pants off, but they cut my shirt off. I should have stuffed my belt in my boots. I also lost my coat. They gave me back my boots and my pants. I got to go buy a new belt. It was fun. I don't get to buy belts very often.

Both the EMT's I rode with were in training, but they had a gal that was in charge. In the ER they put one of those Bair Hugger pods on me blowing hot air. It was kinda nice. "Not bad. You guys throw these out when you're done?"

"No."

I would have taken it home. It was pretty cool. It would be nice for star gazing in the winter—go out in the yard and plug it in.

After we came home that evening, we went across the street to talk with Hubert's son, Ray. He told us Fox News was coming. He had been unaware of much that happened. He had asked his daughter, "I wonder what Dad's doing with the backhoe." They were only aware there was a problem after the ambulance showed up.

That same day, Hubert's generator blew up. Kay started

networking on community groups for a generator. They got them a loaner.

That evening a neighbor brought us pizza for dinner. It was a community thing—this whole event. So many neighbors helped.

When we were eating dinner at about 9:00 or 9:30, we saw a KPTV (local Fox channel) vehicle driving up and down the road. Kay watched the news and saw the interview with the Silverton Fire Chief about the story. It was on AP and in the NY Times. My relatives in Vermont and Arizona heard the story. So many of the facts were wrong. One said that the power was out and Barbara was trying to get water out of the well and fell in. The depth of the well was different in every story.

In talking to Hubert the next day, he said, "The first time we met you said, 'If you ever need anything, come over.'"

I laughed. I wasn't thinking, "Wife is in the well," I was thinking more like, "Can I borrow some propane or a clamp?"

The next day, a reporter came from KOIN 6 news and wanted to interview me. The neighbor, Steve, said to me, "I've got this." He told her Peter was probably at work.

When he was half way into the story I said, "I'm Peter." I told her I wasn't at liberty to answer questions about Barbara. When asked why I went into the well, I said, "What was the option? Someone had to do it."

It took me a couple of weeks to process what happened. Many people asked how I could go into that well. I couldn't understand how anyone could be there and *not* do that. In talking with my family including my father, brother, sisters, aunts and some friends, we concluded that there are two kinds of people: doers and watchers. One of my aunts said, "Good job. It doesn't surprise us."

So many things played into me being the way I am. My Mom died when I was in my early teens. I didn't know how to care for her or help, but I knew I could help Barbara. I went into Outward Bound right out of high school. We had a one week Ropes course with rock climbing and rappelling. I realize that although I work on boilers, I have always worked in healthcare facilities. I care for people and put myself at risk to help. In recent conversations with my Dad, we talked about my Mom for the first time. This experience was an eye opener for my entire family. Everything is interconnected.

7

Phil's Story

Hello, my name is Phil Sowa (no pen name available yet to hide my identity or surely I would use it). Having retired after a career in the U.S. Navy, the decision was make in 2009 to join the Silverton Fire District as a volunteer firefighter. In mid-February, 2021, around noon a 911 page came from Dispatch over my phone: "70YOF has fallen down a well at 3533 Crooked Finger Rd..." or words to that effect. Since that address was located on my way to Station 9 Fire House at Ettlin Loop, I arrived driving my Privately Owned Vehicle (POV). To my surprise the address turned out to be the residence of Barbara and Hubert Hettwer. As I drove up the driveway, Hubert was visible along with some other folks...but no Barbara. The "70YOF down the well" was Barbara. Not good! She was successfully rescued and has recovered very well.

A year or so later, Barbara asked me if I would write a chapter for her book about her rescue and recount my ordeal involving her ordeal. Now you have the opportunity to go through the ordeal again with me. Blame Barbara. This is all her doing.

First, allow me to state my position in all this. This account (for what it's worth) is about my personal experience and is in no way official, not as a spokesman for Silverton Fire District nor any other member thereof. (Pretty lawyerly!) Not being much of a fire fighter myself because of poor hearing accompanied by substandard listening habits, I'm more of a fire fighter mascot, not working on my résumé, embedded in my ways, but with the luxury of rubbing shoulders with the men and women who are seriously involved in the marvelous and admirable profession of being genuine First Responders. (Take a breath).

A word of caution: since this is being penned well over 20 months after the incident occurred, and me being a long-time-qualified-for 10%-senior-citizen discounts and my memory/recall being hidden in all the other benefits of being AARP eligible, some "facts" may not be verifiable or accurate. Artistic license is a wonderful thing (another breath!)

Now, back to the ordeal. I had the honor or burden of being "First on Scene." With Barbara at the bottom of the well, the first agenda on a fire fighter's list is to do a "size up," i.e. determine what is really going on. First, it really is Barbara who is in the hole. This is more than another "Alice Floating Down the Rabbit Hole" fairy tale. It's the real McCoy, not just some smoke investigation or other such thing. Second, she miraculously survived the fall and was conscious and coherent. Third, she sustained injuries to her upper body (extent unknown), maybe her head was fine. Fourth, the well had a rock stem wall about 2 feet high. The well was about 3 to 4 feet across and in sound shape. Info was that it was 50+ feet deep with some 12 feet of water in it (good for breaking a fall). It had some timbers laying across the top, some broken, some not. Next to the well, an old but stout tractor was parked with its bucket positioned over the top of the well opening...(a good start) provided by an on-the-scene-former-fire fighter named Hubert, who was thinking ahead. Fifth, Barbara had been in the water a very long time before she was discovered.

Barbara was chest deep in the water wedged against the opposing wall sides. Earlier someone had dropped the end of a small-sized rope down to her to help her out. It was unlikely she would be able to use it considering her injuries. Barbara had been informing us, in no uncertain terms, she was getting weak and likely to lose her footing. Hypothermia at work. She needed help and needed it now being unable to tread water or stay afloat with upper body injuries. I asked Hubert for a snatch block (pulley) and a good length of rope. He provided both. Someone was going to have to go down in the well and help stabilize Barbara. Me!? (Claustrophobia, go away!) I hung the pulley on the tractor bucket and tested a single strand of Hubert's common, household utility rope by putting my weight on it and bouncing up and down. It held.

Miraculously a young man name Pete showed up donning a light-weight climbing harness similar to what I use in construction. So we had a rope that was not National Fire Protection Association (NFPA) approved for rescue operations and a non-OSHA-approved harness. Good enough. Pete had received some training suited for doing the job with Barbara. I doubled the rope, put it through the pulley and tied about a dozen knots on Pete's harness. With the help of the neighbors, we lowered Pete down to Barbara without dropping him or anything else on Barbara's head. Pete was able to position himself with Barbara to support her and keep her safe. We kept some tension on the rope in order to aid him in holding Barbara in place. Great, we bought some time...for now.

All the time, there was a lot of radio traffic. North battalion chief, Jim, T., along with Mt. Angel fire chief (another Jim T. #451) had arrived. More First Responders and an ambulance with medics arrived on scene. The Rope Rescue Team from

Salem had been activated. That team had all the equipment, training, knowledge, and where-with-all for this rescue.

Stuff was coming together. It was time for the old man (me) to step aside. Things were happening as fast as humanly possible (just not as fast as we wanted). The Salem team did a fantastic job of pulling Barbara out of the well, then Pete. It was a big relief to get eyes on Barbara and see Pete again. She looked like she'd had enough. The fire fighters and ambulance medics did a first rate job handling, treating, and transporting Barbara and hero Pete to the hospital for further care.

Everyone was fortunate that the call turned out as successfully as it did. I am amazed to this day at how important Pete's actions were and at how Barbara's amazing strength and fortitude carried her through it all. The well has been filled in and no longer exists but the memory of it all is still there for many of us.

It's time now to move on to the next 911 call, whatever it may be.

8

Hospital

The ambulance jolted to a stop at the emergency entrance of Salem hospital; as the vehicle's doors opened, the gray sky reappeared. There were a few bumps as I was wheeled into the hospital emergency room. Hubert and his daughter, Maria, were there, seated in chairs to my left. My temperature when I arrived at the hospital had warmed up to 87.7°. Soon the Bair Hugger was around, beneath, and over me. I grew warmer.

They took me for a CT Scan and determined that I had a crushed L3 vertebrae, a cracked sternum, and two broken shoulders. That was the first time I knew I was injured. Looking back, my reaction should have been surprise or sadness, but I felt nothing. Between shock and drugs, my feelings were as numb as my body.

Back in the emergency room, two doctors on my right side had a machine and were looking at my bones in my right arm. I could see the screen. The humerus bone was completely severed just below the ball and completely out of alignment, not even touching the ball. Later I realized how amazing it was that the bone had not broken the skin.

The young doctor aligned my humerus at the direction of the older man. "That's as good as you can get it. Right there."

It didn't hurt when they made that adjustment. I asked what they had given me. They said, "Fentanyl." I looked at Hubert and Maria and laughed, remembering that Fentanyl is a much stronger drug than morphine and had played a part in the death of Michael Jackson. I suppose anything would have resulted in laughter at that time as I was feeling great!

I asked about my clothes. Maria found them in a pile on the floor there in the emergency room. She said she would take them home and wash them. I later found out that she threw them in the washing machine without examining them, but when she took them out, they were shredded. She realized they had cut off my clothes, so she threw them away. I certainly had no memory of my clothes being cut.

I was taken to the 7th floor of Building A, which is the trauma unit. Due to COVID-19 restrictions, I was limited to one visitor per day which covered the 24 hour period from 7:00 a.m. to 7:00 a.m. the following day. However, priests and chaplains came and went freely.

On Friday, my first full day in the hospital, my son, Mark, from Bellevue, Washington, came with food. This is the same Mark who was the baby I held when having my vision of being in a pit. His wife, Steph, spent most of Thursday night cooking for Hubert and me to keep us on our lectin-free, gluten-free, sugar-free, all-natural, low-carb diet. Mark slept on the window seat of my room overnight. I appreciated his comforting presence.

Father Joseph from Saint Joseph's church in Salem came to visit me on Friday. He heard my confession and blessed me with the Anointing of the Sick. Deacon Allen, a chaplain at the hospital, also came and prayed for me.

On Saturday, Father Ralph, my pastor from St. Mary's

in Mount Angel, came to visit. I told him that after I had received the Anointing of the Sick my upper left rib cracked when the nurses were rolling me onto my side. He gave me that blessing again. I told him that I had prayed some prayers in my life including the Saint Bridget prayers and the Chaplet of Divine Mercy, and that, although I was not consistent, those prayers had promises that you would receive Viaticum, last Holy Communion, before dying. I shared with him that I had told God that since there was no priest with me in the well to give me communion, I couldn't die there.

Father Ralph warmly laughed, "I am glad I wasn't there!"

Hubert was my Saturday visitor and brought me several personal items from home. Among them was a book I requested called *Healing Words* by Sylvia Rogers. A friend had loaned it to me, and I had read about half of it. After an explanation of how to use the prayers, the book had chapters on various ailments. While Hubert and I were on a weekend vacation a few months earlier, I had prayed the ones for the skeletal system because my hips and back sometimes hurt. I began reading those prayers every day. They were mostly Scripture about the health of one's bones.

My hospital room had a large picture window with a pleasant view of Bush's Pasture Park. The window sill was crammed with colorful flower arrangements, cards, and balloons. Nurses commented on the abundance. I thought everyone got cards and flowers in the hospital, but they said that was not the case. Friends and relatives comforted me with their words of love and prayer notes.

Sunday was once again Mark's day. On Sunday afternoon, I started having abdominal pains. At first, I didn't think much of it. It started to hurt to urinate and seemed to take a while to get it to happen. I told the nurse I thought I had a UTI. They took a urine sample and many hours later when there were four nurses/CNAs in my room due to my nagging complaints, the results came back negative. I told them there had to be something wrong. Their suggestion was to give me more drugs to kill my pain. I insisted that they figure out what was wrong because I was having surgery on my right shoulder the next morning, and I couldn't possibly have surgery with excruciating pain and a swollen belly.

Finally, one nurse suggested they scan my belly. She got a portable ultrasound machine and saw that my bladder was full. They put in a catheter, which was quite difficult and took an experienced nurse great effort, but soon relieved the pain.

Mark stayed until 7:00 am. Monday morning. I was scheduled for surgery at 10:30. He assumed they would just screw my bones together. They came to get me at 8:30 saying that their first surgery patient had eaten breakfast, so my surgery time changed. They asked if I wanted anti-anxiety medicine, but I declined saying that I was fine. They wheeled me down the hallway into the elevator, then to the surgery floor and into a prep room. Once in that small room with no windows and the door closed, I felt a panic attack coming on.

I've had claustrophobia most of my life. About twelve years earlier, it was so bad that it led to frequent panic attacks. I improved by praying, quitting work, and taking amino acids for my brain (GABA and Taurine) and Valerian root tincture for relaxation. Recent attacks have been rare. I learned to avoid the causes. Many friends have asked how I didn't have a panic attack in the well. It never even entered my mind. According to Pete, I did panic a few times, but he calmed me down. I must have been protected by God and been focused on one thing: survival.

The surgeon came in to discuss the surgery with me which helped distract me from my anxiety. He explained my three options. The first was to do nothing. The second was to screw the bones together. He said that was usually not successful in people over 40 years old. Since they had determined that I have osteopenia, a thinning of the bones, he would not advise that. The third option was a reverse shoulder replacement.

That would put the ball joint on top and the socket below. It would limit my ability in the future to raise my arm above 130°. I chose the third option. The surgeon left the tiny room, and I once again felt the walls closing in.

When the nurse returned, I asked for the anti-anxiety meds. She said she would have to ask the doctor. A wave of frustration came over me. Why could they give me something before I came to the surgery prep room, but not once I was there? The nurse left, and I got more and more distraught and had trouble breathing. Then Deacon Allen walked into the room. I was so happy to see him. He prayed for me, and we talked. Then I was fine.

As it turns out, there was a small slit in the plastic wrapping of some of the surgical parts, and they had to send all the surgical items back to the sanitizing room. They gave me the choice of waiting there or going back to my room. I chose my room and was very relieved to get back to my view of trees and endless sky.

Two hours later, they came back to take me down to surgery again. That time they took me straight into the surgery room. I told them I wanted them to only have happy conversations during the surgery—about flowers and butterflies.

One of the men said, "Well, there's mostly men here."

I said "Okay, you can talk about cars." One of them started talking about a car he had and how he had taken it apart and struggled putting it back together. I fell asleep being entertained by his story.

I woke up in a huge room with two people standing on each side of me. I felt fine. They soon took me back to my room.

When I talked to Mark on the phone and told him that I had a reverse shoulder replacement and would never be able to raise my arm over 130°, he was upset and said, "Mom, how will you swim?" I told him I could dog paddle.

When I was in the well, I only thought about getting out.

There was no blood that I could see, and the frigid water numbed me so that I had no idea how serious my injuries were. I actually had five broken bones, a badly sprained left ankle, a scraped back from pressing against the rock wall, a gash on my knee, and a bruised right leg (purple from hip to ankle).

Several times a CNA came in, pulled back the sheet and gasped, "Your leg is all bruised!" They see accident victims all the time. I realized my leg must be very bad if they were shocked.

My scraped back would leak a little blood on the sheets. They decided to put a Chux under my back. Only two nurses offered to put some cream on my back. The staff was more concerned with keeping me alive than fixing my owies. I also had a bad scab on my right knee that was never treated. The scab came off two months later leaving a purple indentation.

One day while lying in bed, a man entered my room. "Mark!" I instantly recognized him. The uniform helped. He was my ambulance caregiver.

"We just brought a patient here, and I wanted to come see how you're doing."

"I'm all right. Did you have many hypothermia patients before me?"

"Nope," he shook his head, "You were my first."

I'm glad I didn't know that in the ambulance! I realized that I probably gave him a good scare. His concern for me was another blessing.

I had a visitor every day, some relatives, some neighbors, some friends. My regular Wednesday visitor was a friend who brought me yogurt so I could mix my much-needed collagen in it. Steph either brought meals or sent them through Hubert. The meals were so good that nurses wanted the recipes. There were blueberry or carrot muffins for breakfast with an egg bake filled with sausage, spinach and cheese. Dinner was salmon, roasted red potatoes, and asparagus, or roast beef with potatoes and carrots. Two friends bought me good, comfortable slip-on shoes with ankle support and non-slip soles. Maria and my friends also bought me clothing that would slip on easily over my arms with immobile shoulders.

Both my arms were in slings. They were only removed to dress me, for manipulation by a therapist, or when I was awake to try to straighten them. I would remove the right sling and lay my arm on a pillow as straight as it could go. My arms were getting permanently bent, but the right arm was worse. At first, therapy was in bed in the trauma unit with leg exercises and massages and slight movement of my arms. It has been a slow process to recover. I have worked hard but very cautiously. I was slow to get out of a hospital gown and into regular clothing. Every new step took coaxing from the hospital staff, but when I was convinced to try something, I tried hard and succeeded.

A few days after surgery, a lady came in to talk with me about where to go when I left the hospital. I said, "I am *not* going to a skilled nursing facility." She told me there were many options available, and she could check into where there were openings. I repeated my adamant opinion. I told her I would rather go home with no care. I knew with COVID restrictions that no visitors were allowed in nursing facilities. I asked how much physical therapy I would receive there. She said a few hours a week. I reiterated my stance. She then explained that the hospital had a rehab unit. However, you had to be able to tolerate 3.5 hours of therapy per day. I couldn't even stand yet! I asked about the visiting policy—it was the same as the unit I was in. I told her I would do it. After a week and a half on the trauma floor, I was moved to Rehab on the fourth floor of Building B.

~~~~~~~~~~~~~~~~~~~~~~~~

Among the cards I received while in the hospital was one from a friend, Caryl, who had led me in healing prayer every week for a year. Near the end of that year, we added a trauma prayer. When Caryl heard about my accident, she wrote out by hand the trauma prayer specifically for my situation and mailed it to me in the hospital. For two months after falling in the well, I prayed that every day along with the Rosary plus the *Healing Words* prayers.

Several times depression swept through my heart. Occasionally, I questioned my decision to have the shoulder replacement. I would be hindered in movement for the rest of my life. I come from a family of strong bones where no one had ever broken a bone. It probably would have healed up by itself. I would pray at those times and agree with God that I made the best decision and all would be well.

~~~~~~~~~~~~~~~~~~~~~

There were two doctors in that unit who alternated, working one week on and the next week off. They were both excellent and did daily rounds. My first week in Rehab was Dr. Pavlik's week. He was a delight. After a few minutes of his routine doctor questions, he would sit down and chat with me. We had great conversations about our family histories, education, and good literature.

Each day as therapists tried to stand me up, my blood pressure dropped, and they had to put me back down on my bed or chair. I did therapy in bed or in a wheel chair. Dr. Pavlik decided that I needed TED hose—those dreadfully tight socks that get rid of swelling and push the fluid up your legs. I already had leg pumps on while in bed and didn't mind that. I had put TED hose on others before and knew I didn't want them. They are hard to get on and the mere thought of them gave me a panic attack. My claustrophobia kicks in when I am locked into something that I can't get off or open (a locked car door, a necklace with a difficult clasp, etc.). Dr. Pavlik said he would order the TED hose for me. I told him I didn't want them, and I would pray that God would fix my blood pressure so I wouldn't have to wear them. He said that was fine but he would order them anyway. The next day, the TED hose still hadn't come to my room and my blood pressure dropped when I stood up. I prayed some more. The following day, I stood up and my blood pressure remained stable. The TED hose came, but I never wore them.

My therapists were awesome. My physical therapist was usually a young woman named Susanna. She pushed me to work harder than I liked. She had me walking while she held a Gait belt around my waist and had Hubert or my friend-of-the-day pushing a wheelchair behind me in case I got dizzy. She had me do a comfortable seated bicycle to strengthen my legs. One day another therapist, Angela, came. I asked where my regular was. Angela said Susanna was a student and had finished her time there at the hospital. I was amazed that a student had been so excellent. I continued therapy with Angela. She taught me to go up and down two stairs and get in and out of a car.

The occupational therapists were great also. Gail was especially good at making devices to improve the quality of a patient's life. Since I had very limited shoulder motion, I couldn't reach the bed tray with either hand no matter where they placed it. Gail made a cup holder out of the bottom half of a plastic urinal, with a ring punched through it. She hung it from the bed rail and I kept my water cup in it. John was great at massaging my arm, especially my right arm with the shoulder replacement. It was stiff and swollen. He could get it moving and get the swelling down.

Hospital staff began talking to me about going home. The date seemed fluid. I arranged for my daughter-in-law, Steph, to come to my house on Thursday. She had volunteered to be my caregiver. The hospital told me on Tuesday that I was going home on Wednesday. I refused. I said I couldn't because I wouldn't have a caregiver until Thursday. They changed my release date.

I was often asked about my pain level. I didn't really have much pain, not while falling, not in the well. Only in the ambulance. Not from the surgery, not too much from therapy. The only sharp pain was from my back, sometimes coming on suddenly and also causing neuropathic pains in my right thigh, which could be sudden and stabbing. Other than that, it was just discomfort. I did need more than Tylenol to sleep at night, just to get comfortable. Considering what my body endured, that is really nothing.

I had excellent care at Salem Hospital. That may be due to my insistence on certain issues. I had full command of my mental faculties. I regularly thanked the nurses, CNAs, and the cleaning crew. I do have sympathy for patients who can't express what they need and those who are so miserable that they forget to be kind.

THE WOMAN IN THE WELL ~ 59

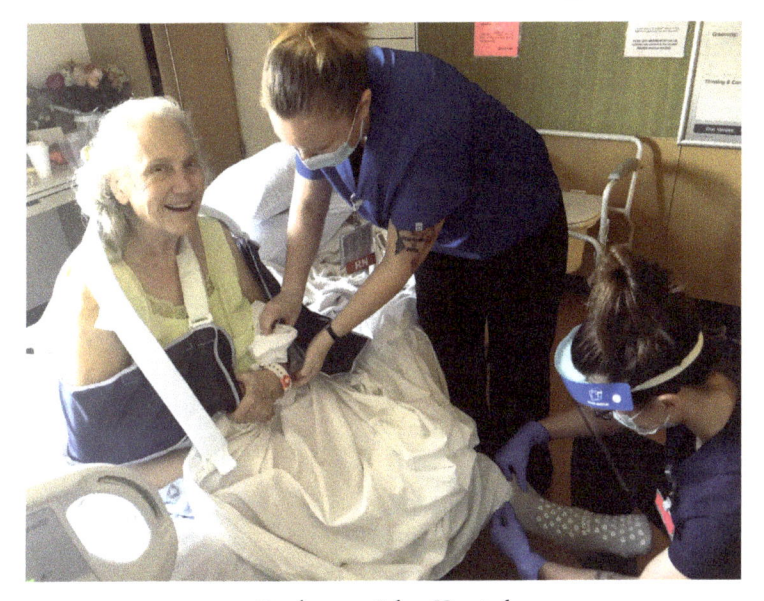

Good care at Salem Hospital

Flowers & Cards from thoughtful friends & relatives

9

Jeana's Story

Smoke hung in the air Sunday morning as a sobering reminder of the fires that swept through the hills surrounding our area. The Beachie Creek fire, one of the largest in the country for 2020, and the Lionshead fire that swept down the Santiam Canyon, both claiming homes, businesses, land, and lives merged above Scotts Mills days after Labor Day. Thanks to local volunteers, our small community, which was evacuated for nearly a week, was saved with only a minimum loss of homes. Unlike the towns of Detroit, Mill City, and their surrounding area, there was no loss of life.

On Sundays after church we usually stand outside and talk for a while with others. Hubert had already gone to the car and was waiting for Barbara. While she was walking to the car I said I needed to talk to her about something. She said, "If it's quick because we have company coming for breakfast, Mark and his family. There's something I need to tell you too."

When I finished, she told me that she had been standing on top of the old well trying to make a call out on her cell phone as she usually did because that's the best place for reception when the phone lines aren't working. They were down because the electrical lines were shut off due to the fire. She heard the timbers crack and felt it give a little. She had told Hubert about it, and he said he would fix it but hadn't done anything yet. Barbara expressed her fear. "If I had fallen in, it would be terrible with my fear of enclosed spaces." She reminded me of her fear even in airplanes.

I said, "Let's pray about that." Barbara said, "Okay, if it's not too long." so we began. Barbara started by praying in tongues opening to the Holy Spirit.

Then I prayed, "Lord, we praise You and thank You for Barbara's life and for keeping her from falling into the well. Please take away any fear and trauma from that." then I said, "Repeat after me:

Heavenly Father I turn to you and open my heart...I choose to forgive Hubert for not repairing and taking care of this right away...I forgive him and release him to you...Please forgive me for giving into fear and trauma...and because You forgive me, I forgive myself...and release myself from all guilt, blame, and shame...In the name of Jesus, and by the power of His Blood, I cancel Satan's authority over me...

I command you fear, 'Go!'...
trauma, 'Go!'...
fear of what might happen, 'Go!'...
control, 'Go!'...
un-trust of God, 'Go!'...
self hatred, 'Go!'...
Come Holy Spirit...
Fill me with Your grace...
with peace...
trust...
faithfulness...
love...
I ask You to break every trigger from this memory...

every thought...
every emotion...
every sight...
every sound...
every smell...
every sensation...
every flavor...

Please, break these triggers, heal my heart, heal my body, and renew my mind. And show me Your truth about this." This is the same prayer Barbara posted on Facebook on March 6, after falling into the well.

After a time of silence I said I got the sense that God was going to allow her to fall in. Her eyes widened in dismay, and she said, "How can that be since we just prayed against it? I don't think it would be His will for that to happen."

I reminded her that God allows evil so that He can bring a greater good out of it. And that "what is intended for evil, God uses for good." (Genesis 50:20) and "All things work for good for those who love the Lord and are called according to His purposes." (Romans 8:28)

So, we prayed fervently. "Jesus, we pray again that Barbara would NOT fall into that well. But, we also pray, that if You allow it, that You would be right there with her. That You would fill her with Your peace that surpasses all understanding, O Prince of Peace. And because of that peace, she would know, that she knows, that she knows, that You are with her. Surprise her with the strength to endure and love for life which Your presence brings. I also ask, Lord, that if You allow this, all who are involved would be amazed. That there would be conversions, testimonies, and Barbara would even write a book about it so that everyone who hears of it would come closer to You, Lord Jesus. All for Your glory, O God! And Jesus, [I put my hand on her forehead] I pray that You would cover Barbara's mind, body, soul, and intellect with Your Most Precious Blood and give her peace and rest in You for this possibility with such trust that, if it be Your will, she would no longer even think about it. And if that is the case, please bring it back to her memory at a time of Your visitation so that she may give glory to You. Jesus, we trust in You! Amen."

10

Recovery

Hubert came to pick me up on Thursday, March 11, at the end of a full three weeks in the hospital. Two of the hospital staff wheeled me out along with a cart overflowing with my collection of flowers. I was nervous on the drive home. I had my two slings on and held my arms carefully in front of me. I watched the road and warned Hubert of any road obstacles. All I could think of was how much it would hurt if the airbag hit me.

When we arrived home, Steph took over. She was amazing. She cooked all the food, bathed and dressed me, took me to physical therapy, did our grocery shopping, and kept a baby monitor in her room so I could call her in the middle of the night to go potty. Steph also bought me clever items online that made life easier such as hospital gowns that looked like regular clothing, a short stool for me to get into bed, an electric toothbrush, a new landline phone with a headset, and an electric razor so she could shave my legs and underarms.

Steph would stay for at least a week, then drive four hours

home and care for her family for three or four days. She left us prepared food in the refrigerator and freezer. While home, she did her family's grocery shopping and planned their meals, then returned to me. Her husband and mother took care of the four children when she was with me.

When Steph was home, I had a great caregiver named Rosa for about five hours each day, except Sundays. Rosa was excellent and gave great arm and back massages. Hubert was my Sunday helper.

A difficult time was when a friend, Jeana, called on the phone when I was still in the hospital and was very excited to remind me of a conversation we'd had several months earlier. She said I had told her that I stood on the wood on top of the well and heard it crack. At that time she prayed that if I fell in the well I wouldn't have claustrophobia. I didn't believe her. If that conversation had happened I would have remembered. We pray together often, and I knew she would have prayed for me to *not* fall in the well. How silly to pray that I wouldn't have claustrophobia *in* the well. I told Jeana she must have dreamed that.

After I was home, we discussed this a few more times. Jeana has convinced me that it did happen. She remembers where we were standing in the church parking lot during our conversation and the smoke in the air due to the autumn fires. For a while, this was very depressing. I have never had the greatest memory, but I do remember major events. If a frightening incident happened, then I told a friend, and she prayed about it, I would remember. If what Jeana related to me had happened, that would mean my horrendous experience was completely avoidable because I had been warned. It seemed that God had wiped that completely out of my mind. I truly struggled to understand how this could have been allowed by God, even after a warning. A wave of depression came over me every time I thought about this.

Hubert and my grandkids have told me that everyone

knew not to stand on the well. I really don't remember that. How could that be? God, in His mercy, answered my friend's prayer, and I didn't have claustrophobia while I was alone in the well. I have always relied upon God, but for the first two hours in the well I *completely* relied upon Him. I had nothing but God, His love, and His will for me. Despite my foolishness and lack of wisdom, God used this situation to draw me closer to Him

Quote from *Trustful Surrender to Divine Providence* by Father Jean Baptiste Saint-Jure, written in the 17th century: "God, as we have said, wishes to make you see your own faults, to humble you, deprive you of what you possess, in order to free you from vice and lead you to virtue...Do not let ourselves be troubled when we are sometimes beset by adversity, for we know that it is meant for our spiritual welfare and carefully proportioned to our needs."

~~~~~~~~~~~~~~~~~~~~~

About a month after my event, my son, David, came to visit from Southern California. He had been calling but would have had difficulty getting away from work, and he knew Mark was by my side. David and Mark went across the street to meet Pete. They thanked him for saving their mother's life! They wanted to hear Pete's version of the story and were engrossed in the details for about an hour. They reimbursed Pete for his ambulance and hospital bill even though he tried several times to decline. I realized that my boys are now men.

Each day I made progress. Normal activities such as putting lotion on my arms were a great advance. I needed much help with bathroom activities. Even after I could go by myself, like a big girl, I couldn't pull my pants up in the back because my right arm couldn't reach behind me at all due to the construction of the reverse shoulder. I proudly announced to the family when I could pull up my pants in the front, but for months, I would toddle to the kitchen and ask someone to pull up the back of my pants. The first day I took a shower alone and shampooed my hair was exciting.

In addition to physical therapy, my doctor used several modern therapies to aid in my bones healing. His techniques not only helped my bones grow together solidly but also my vertebrae in my back to heal so there was no longer neuropathy in my leg.

After six months, I was doing amazingly well. I could dress myself, drive, and take care of all normal life duties. Strangers assumed I was fine. I continued physical therapy exercises every day on my own to increase my strength and range of motion.

My neighbor and I got back to our exercise routine. When I couldn't do a movement, I would watch her and imagine doing it. We did water exercise in the local pool occasionally. My first time back in the water, I pushed off the bottom towards the deeper end of the pool and started to swim. I nearly drowned! My arms didn't work. I quickly kicked and paddled backwards until I could touch the bottom and stand up. I have since learned to do a modified breast stroke and a left side stroke.

44 days post-well, trying to look normal for Easter

11

Thoughts To Ponder

An old joke: *My friend keeps saying, "Cheer up, man, it could be worse. You could be stuck underground in a hole full of water." I know he means well.*

I pondered the questions I was often asked:

- Why am I alive?
- How did I not hit my head? Almost every nurse asked me this.
- Why didn't my legs get broken?
- Why didn't I get water up my nose?
- Why didn't any broken bones push through my skin?
- Why didn't I get any bad cuts that would have caused severe bleeding?
- Why didn't I die from hypothermia?

- What made the neighbor in Idaho think to text Allen?
- Why was the only rope available (Pete's red rope) exactly the right length?
- How did Allen's phone work in his pasture where he has no service?
- Why did Hubert go to Pete instead of Ray, his son, next door?

I later found out that I was in the well alone for two hours. The temperature of the water was 43°-44°. At that temperature exhaustion or unconsciousness can occur in less than an hour. Survival is one to three hours. Pete was with me for almost two hours.

Another poem by Judy Gabriel
There once was a woman quite old
Who fell in a well very cold.
We wondered would she tell
Why she fell in the well,
And now the story's been told.

12

Preparation

Many people, if not all, that have heard my story have said they would not have survived. I have pondered what enabled me to withstand the fall, the cold water, the dark pit, the trauma, the surgery, and the months of rehab. I can see that the first seventy years of my life contributed to my survival. I believe this is true for most people. If one cooperates with God's teachings and His grace even to a reasonable degree (no one can do this perfectly), He will lead you in paths that prepare you for your future—which only He knows.

I grew up in a Catholic family with a mom and dad and two older siblings. We were sent to a Catholic school. I had the gift of faith from the time I can remember. I never doubted there was a good God who loved me, created me in His image, and had a plan for my life. We learned certain prayers in school and that included the prayers that constitute the Rosary. It begins with a statement of faith which caused me to ponder those tenets regularly. Each day of the week is assigned five mysteries for meditation. Those are mostly events in the earthly life of Jesus. The ten Hail Mary prayers count out the time to ponder each event. Therefore, it is a wonderful meditative prayer focused on Jesus. This helped me focus in the well when my mind was foggy.

A standard response in Catholic circles to any kind of pain is, "Offer it up." This means to offer up your pain or suffering in union with the suffering of Christ on the cross often for the Poor Souls in Purgatory, or for any intention. In recent years, every time I prayed, I prayed for my children, grandchildren and godchildren. Since my sister passed away, my prayers for children and grandchildren have included hers also. So in the well it was natural for me to offer up my suffering for these loved ones and Hubert.

I had lived in paralyzing fear for most of my childhood. Discussions with my mom and her sister had led us to conclude that my mom's fears stemmed from her mother living in terrible fear while she was pregnant with my mom. They lived in an unsavory neighborhood of New York City, and my grandmother had to walk up a dark stairwell to their third floor apartment. The apartment was also dark due to her husband's eye sensitivities. My mother inherited many fears, and I seemed to be born with fear surrounding me. I relied upon God when fear would overtake me. For example, lying in bed at night as a child, I experienced worms crawling all over me. They weren't long earthworms but fat, inch-long worms. There were none in reality, but I *knew* they were there and could feel them. I prayed, and God covered my entire body with an acrylic-type shield. The worms were still there, but I couldn't feel them, and they couldn't touch me. This prepared me to trust God to relieve my fears and make unbearable situations tolerable.

When I was in the sixth grade, my parents decided to put a swimming pool in our back yard. My grandmother was an excellent swimmer and had tried to teach me to swim, but I always sank. Both my parents were smooth swimmers with perfect form. For my safety, my parents made me take swimming lessons at the local YMCA. After that, I swam often in our pool. I was like a fish. I enjoyed diving off the board and perfected my jack-knife. At the public pool, I dove off the high dive. I had no fear of water.

After Mark was born, I must have had postpartum depression, but never thought of it in those terms. My mother-in-law invited me to a Life In The Spirit Seminar. Once a week for a month, ladies shared their experiences of God's love, provision, and protection. I had always believed God created and loved us, but had rarely experienced His love in a palpable way. At the end of the month, I had the ladies pray for me to be fully immersed in the Holy Spirit. When I began letting simple sounds out of my mouth, joy and laughter exploded. From that day forward, I prayed in tongues—a language that was all my own, given to me by God. Although I couldn't translate each word of my language, I knew whether I was interceding for someone or praising God. Praying in tongues enables me to pray when I can't think of what to say. This was invaluable in the well when my frozen brain could no longer put a coherent thought together.

After that infilling with the Holy Spirit in a powerful way, I had an insatiable desire to read the Bible. I would get up at night to nurse Mark (yes, the same one who sat with me in the hospital over forty years later). Afterward, I would lay him down on the couch next to me and read the Bible. One of those nights, I had the experience with Psalm 40 where Jesus reached down to me to rescue me out of the pit.

By 1980, I watched Trinity Broadcasting Network regularly and became involved in Women's Aglow, an interdenominational Christian group. Through Aglow I spent a summer as a 700 Club telephone prayer counselor. All of these experiences widened and deepened my prayer life. I learned to take authority over negative forces and quote Scripture as a powerful spiritual weapon. I spoke Scripture and truth and not my fears. Thus in the well I spoke, "I shall live and not die."

In 2015, I went to Caryl of Wellspring Ministries for weekly prayer. She taught me to recognize the forces that buffeted me and how to command them to depart in the Name of Jesus. She is the one who sent me the trauma prayer that I used daily in the hospital and that Jeana prayed in the parking lot. All of these experiences combined to enable my survival!

13

Lessons I Learned Well & FAQ

- When accidents happen, no one needs to be blamed. I could blame myself as Hubert had recently said, "I should change those boards. They are probably rotting from all this rain." After all, *I am* the one who stood on the well. I could blame Hubert because he didn't replace the boards. I could blame the local fire departments because they didn't get me out sooner. Then, there is the most common One to blame—God. If he hadn't created gravity, I wouldn't have fallen. Of course, the futility of all this is evident. None of that would change my current reality.
- A sense of humor is a wonderful medicine. Studies have shown that laughter releases endorphins. This deadens pain and supports healing. The hospital staff

had some great comments. Every time they would say, "Well,..." they would stop and says, "Ooops! Guess I shouldn't say that." One therapist came bounding into my room one day and said, "I have a name for your book! *Well, Well, Well.*" Someone else quipped, "Well Diving is going to be the new Olympic sport."

- Don't be too skinny. You never know when you're going to need that adipose tissue to insulate you and buoy you up.
- Don't be too fat. You never know when you may fall into a pit. You wouldn't want to be so big that you are wedged in and stuck. You wouldn't want there to be no room for your neighbor to join you in your abyss.
- Have a close relationship to God. Someday He may be your only companion and hope.
- Be kind to your neighbors. You may need them to save your life. Bring cookies to the new neighbors!
- Good people can have different views and opinions depending on their life experiences and perspective (above ground or 40' down).
- Stay in good shape and be as healthy as possible. You may need every ounce of that strength and health to survive an accident.
- Don't second guess your unchangeable decisions. Am I better off with my reverse total shoulder replacement made of chromate cobalt, titanium, and polyethylene rather than just screws? I don't know.
- If you're disabled, you can still be useful but in different ways. You can have a huge impact on the world

by praying. You also give others a chance to exercise their compassion.
- If you have a friend in the hospital, be sure you are his advocate for good care if he can't do it himself and send cards and flowers!

FAQ:

- Was there any warning before you fell in the well such as cracking sound? *No, none*
- Did your feet ever touch the bottom of the well? *No, not that I noticed.*
- Did your life pass before your eyes? *No*
- How cold did you feel in the water? *I didn't really feel cold, such as teeth chattering or shivering. I was mentally aware that the water was very cold, which I knew was dangerous.*
- How much pain were you in when you were in the well? *Very little pain. My back ached and my right shoulder hurt. I solved the problems by dipping my right shoulder in the water. The water was so cold, it numbed the pain.*
- What is the purpose for which God baptized you anew? *To tell the world He is real, loves us, and saved me.*
- Why did you tell about the fires and ice storm in a book about falling in a well? *To give a feel for our daily life and some of the recent unique events that we had experienced. It showed how our neighbors pull together in any and every emergency, which is what happened when I fell in the well.*

Epilogue

Since these events, life has been perfect, right? Well, no. On Sunday, June 6, 2021, I lost my new wedding ring. I looked through the bed covers, pulling each layer apart and shaking it. I am always amazed when I lose something (which happens often) and a friend says, "Where did you lose it?" If I knew where I lost it, it wouldn't be lost! I sadly went to church ringless.

It was the Feast of Corpus Christi. On that Sunday, we have a procession outside with prayer stations. Each person carries a candle in a safe votive container. When we came back into the church, I entered the pew first, then Hubert. I still couldn't get out of a chair easily so I kept a folded blanket on my pew seat to make it higher. I turned my head to look at the seat to be sure my rear end would land on the blanket.

Swoosh! Flames shot up the right side of my head. My hair had hit the candle flame and was on fire! I don't remember what I did with my candle. I shouted "Hubert, my hair is on fire!" and simultaneously put both hands over my hair and put out the flames. There was no ruckus in church. The fire was out, and Mass went on as though nothing had happened. That's hillfolk for you: fire was out, everything was okay. After Mass, a couple of people asked if I was all right. When I got home, I saw some white mess on the top of my shoe. Hubert agreed it looked like bird droppings. I cleaned my shoe. I told Hubert and my brother that they had to make breakfast. I was going to take a shower and attempt to wash my hair to see what was left of it. What a rude day!

After my shower and breakfast, I went to my comfy spot sitting on my bed with my back against the headboard and called Mark for sympathy.

He was playing the "son" role to perfection. "Oh, Mom, that's so terrible."

But halfway through my sad tale of woe, he quit responding. I realized the call had dropped. After several tries, we connected again. I had to laugh at the absurdity of even my sympathy call failing. While I was relating the story of my ring, I looked on the bed and there it was! Because my hair is curly, the burned chunks washed out and it wasn't that noticeable. The next day I realized that part of my mask (required in church by COVID-19 rules) had also burned! The white stuff wiped off my shoe.

Whew! Glad that's over with. From now on, life will be fine.

Well, not quite...On Saturday, October 9, 2021, a little after midnight, the Wilco building in Mt. Angel went up in flames. My brother owned that property. All four old historic feed and seed buildings including two towers were incinerated, destroying four successful businesses leasing space there. Two food carts that St. John Bosco High School uses as Oktoberfest booths burned also. Those are the main source of fundraising for our school. I began working full time to help my brother and the school.

On January 10, 2022, I arrived at my brother's house to find he had died in bed. He was a wonderful big brother. He was the best uncle, teaching kids to work hard and play hard as he did. He was the president of 20 non-profits in his lifetime. The world and I miss him dreadfully.

Bob, Mark & Steph with their 4 children

Epilogue ~ 79

Uncle Bob with nephews -- lunch break while remodeling Oktoberfest booth

Uncle Bob teaching kids to relax fishing in his pond

Author's Notes

A huge thank you and heartfelt gratitude to God, Hubert, Pete, helpful neighbors, three fire departments, and all 35 people who were at my house on February 18, 2021. I am also blessed to have had good care from ambulance attendants, nurses, CNAs, doctors, and therapists, Mark and Steph with their supportive family, David, Rosa, and friends who visited me in the hospital. Thanks also to those who helped me hone my writing skills (such as they are) especially Marianne, Marsha, Donna, Kate, Laurie, Jo, Steph, Judy, and Kathleen.

Some names have been changed by personal request or because they have no idea they are mentioned in my book. Many names are real from those who gave permission for their name to be used.

My time alone in the well was long and grueling. The chapter relating my experience drags on and on. It seemed interminable to me. I did have the realization at that time that it was a type of baptism and have pondered this since then.

"Through Baptism the Christian is sacramentally assimilated to Jesus, who in his own baptism anticipates his death and resurrection. The Christian must enter into this mystery of humble self-abasement and repentance, go down into the water with Jesus in order to rise with him, be reborn of water and the Spirit so as to become the Father's beloved son in the Son and walk in newness of life."

(2000, Catechism of the Catholic Church: Revised in Accordance with the Official Latin Text Promulgated by Pope John Paul II. Washington, DC: United States Catholic Conference. Para. 537)

Printed in the USA
CPSIA information can be obtained
at www.ICGtesting.com
LVHW051022221024
794501LV00020B/510

The Good Book Also Says...

Books by BEN MILDER

Light Verse

The Fine Art of Prescribing Glasses Without Making a Spectacle
  of Yourself   (1979)

The Good Book Says . . . : Light Verse to Illuminate the Old Testament   (1995)

The Good Book Also Says . . . : Numerous Humorous Poems Inspired by
  the New Testament   (1999)

Prose

On the Shoulders of Giants: A History of Ophthalmology at Washington
  University   (1999)

The Good Book Also Says...

*Numerous Humorous Poems
Inspired by the New Testament*

Ben Milder

TIME BEING BOOKS
POETRY IN SIGHT AND SOUND
St. Louis, Missouri

Copyright © 1999 by Ben Milder

All rights reserved under International and Pan-American Copyright Conventions. No part of this book shall be reproduced in any form (except by reviewers for the public press) without written permission from the publisher:

Time Being Books®
10411 Clayton Road
St. Louis, Missouri 63131

Time Being Books® is an imprint of Time Being Press®
St. Louis, Missouri

Time Being Press® is a 501(c)(3) not-for-profit corporation.

Time Being Books® volumes are printed on acid-free paper, and binding materials are chosen for strength and durability.

ISBN 1-56809-060-9 (Hardcover)
ISBN 1-56809-061-7 (Paperback)

Library of Congress Cataloging-in-Publication Data:

Milder, Benjamin, 1915–
    The Good Book also says— : numerous humorous poems inspired by the New Testament / Ben Milder.— 1st ed.
      p.   cm. — (Poetry in sight and sound)
    ISBN 1-56809-060-9 (alk. paper) — ISBN 1-56809-061-7 (pbk. : alk. paper)
    1. Bible. N.T.—History of Biblical events—Poetry. 2. Humorous poetry, American.   I. Title. II. Series.
PS3563.I37159 G65   1999
811'.54—dc21   99-049121

Cover art and illustrations by Amour Krupnik. Courtesy of the artist.
Book design and typesetting by Sheri L. Vandermolen
Manufactured in the United States of America

First Edition, first printing (1999)

Acknowledgments

The reader of a book may assume that the creative process ends when the author's manuscript is turned over to the publisher. The truth is that the end product is the result of a number of further creative efforts.

For these contributions, it is a pleasure to express my thanks and appreciation to Jerry Call, Editor in Chief of Time Being Books, to Sheri L. Vandermolen, Senior Editor, and to my friend and fellow poet, Louis Daniel Brodsky, for his advice and counsel.

I should also like to thank the many members of the clergy who have provided guidance and support in the preparation of this manuscript.

The biblical passages quoted in this volume were taken from The Holy Bible, Revised Standard Version (New York: Thomas Nelson and Sons, 1953).

for Mike, Barry, Mort, and Larry,
who have been blessed with the Lord's gift of humor

Contents

Introduction A Word from the Author *xv*
Preface Doing the Lord's Work 19

The Gospels

Matthew

1:1, etc.	The Begats	23
2:1, etc.	Herod the Horrid	24
3:4	They Must Be Finger-Lickin' Good	25
4:3–4	A Piece of Cake	26
4:23–24	No Appointment Needed	27
5:5	No Closing Costs	28
5:28	Let Thy Lust Rust	29
6:3–4	A Code of Alms	30
7:15	Would You Follow a Prophet Who Looks like Ewe?	31
13:57	. . . Except in His Own Country	32
14:6–8	Odious Herodias	33
14:17, etc.	Catering to the Masses	34
19:6	Tying the Marriage — Not	35
19:23	The Tithes That Bind	36
19:24	Preposterous?	37
22:14	Where the Elite Meet to Eat	38
22:39	Love Thy Neighbor	39
25:14, etc.	Score: Bulls 5; Bears 0	40

Mark

2:16–17	Break Bread with the IRS?	41
3:9, etc.	A Franchised Operation	42
5:25, etc.	Not Typed and Cross-Matched?	43
6:47–48	Walking on Water	44
7:1–2	Look, Ma — No Hans	46
7:32, 35	If I Could Just Heal the Deaf and Dumb	47
11:15	No Place for a Pigeon	48

Luke

1:13, 31	Christmas Is a Two-Day Holiday	49
3:14	I Wish My Office Staff Would Reread Luke	50
5:3	Ship-to-Shore Communication	51
5:4, etc.	This Is No Fish Story	52
5:36	When You Have Your Back to the Wall	53
6:26	Every Sycophantic Antic	54
6:27	Love Your Enemies	55
6:29	Or Put Up Your Dukes?	56
6:31	Those Things That I'd Do unto Others	57
6:37	Judge and Jury	58
10:8	Please, Sir, May I Have Some More?	59
10:23	A Spectacle Dialectical	60
11:9	Seek and Ye Shall Find	61
12:3	Wherein It Is Revealed That Lips Are Never Sealed	63
12:37	Be Sure It's Not Decaffeinated	64
13:30	The Human Race	65

John

2:7–9	Turning Water to Wine	66
3:8–9	Where the Wind Blows, CNN Knows	67
7:14–15	Better Late Than Never	68
11:17, etc.	Lazarus, Come Out	69

Acts of the Apostles

Acts

16–28	I Wish I'd Been Paul's Travel Agent	73
1:26	The Roll of the Dice	74
2:4	Men Spoke in Tongues	76
2:16–17	Old Men Dream Dreams	77
4:32, etc.	Would a Real-Estate Salesman Lie to You?	78
5:3, etc.	Down to Our Last Three Ananiases	79
5:18–19	Absquatulate?	80

9:25	A Tisket, a Tasket, a Very Welcome Basket	*81*
11:4–6	No Fancy Linen on the Table?	*82*
12:21–23	Coming to Terms with Worms	*83*
13:1, etc.	Simeon Who Was Called Niger	*84*
15:1, etc.	Maybe Something Less Surgical?	*85*
19:19	The Magic Art of Turning Money to Ashes	*86*

The Epistles

Romans

1:22–23	Their Prayers Were for the Birds	*89*
1:26–27	Keep Your Passion Old-Fashioned	*90*
7:2	The Man of Her Dreams	*91*
10:11–12	Knishes and Spanokopita	*92*
10:15	With My Feet for Locomotion	*93*
11:18, 21	Getting to the Root of the Matter	*95*
13:1, etc.	Go Right to the Top	*97*
13:6	Let Us Kneel and Pay	*98*

I Corinthians

6:18	After You've Eliminated All Those Sins That Are X-Rated	*99*
7:4	I'm a Vassal in My Castle	*101*
7:8–9	But Can He Drive at Night?	*102*
7:36–38	You Could Stay Engaged Forever	*103*
9:9	An Oxymoron	*104*
12:14, etc.	The Ankle Bone's Connected to the Shin Bone	*105*
14:33–35	How Times Have Changed!	*106*
16:1–2	Ten, or Even More, Percent	*107*

II Corinthians

9:2–5	Give Until It Hurts	*108*
9:7	If You'd Be in God's Good Graces, Put a Smile upon Your Faces	*109*

10:10	Paul Puts It in Writing *110*
11:14–15	The Devil Wears Many Disguises *111*
12:14	Child Support *112*

Ephesians
4:26	If You're Hotheaded, Cool It *113*
5:13	Light Verse *114*
6:5, 9	The CEO vs. the CIO *115*

Colossians
| 2:16 | Even When You Get a Bum Steer *116* |
| 3:20–21 | Spare the Rod? How Odd of God! *117* |

I Thessalonians
| 4:10–11 | Things May Not Be Too Rosy If You're Nosy *118* |
| 5:15 | Housecleaning *119* |

I Timothy
2:11–12	The Silent Sex? Aw, C'mon! *120*
4:4	Broccoli Is Good? *121*
5:23	Any Port in a Storm *122*
6:10	The Root of All Evils *123*

Titus
| 2:6 | When Your Hormones Are Aflame *124* |

Hebrews
5:13–14	Some Sour Notes About Milk *125*
11:11–12	Faith? Viagra? Both? *126*
13:4	The Marriage Bed *127*
13:5	Just Be Happy with Your Lot *128*

James
2:1–3	The Front-Row Pews *129*
2:14	Grab a Hammer *130*
3:8	For Every Poison, There Is an Antidote *131*

I Peter
    3:1–2   Be Submissive to Your Husbands?   *132*
    3:7   That Was Then, This Is Now   *133*

I John
    4:1   Dial 1-800-2BSAVED   *134*
    5:16–17   Not All Sinning Is the Same   *135*

Jude
    16   Loudmouthed Boasters, Turn to Jude   *136*

Revelation

Revelation
    1:10–11   Put It in Writing   *139*
    6:7–8   Behold, a Pale Horse   *140*
    8:2, etc.   Not Even Louie Armstrong Ever Blew His Horn So Hard   *141*
    13:1–2   The Loch Ness Monster?   *142*
    16:1, etc.   The Seven Bowls of God's Wrath   *143*
    16:12   He's Gonna Dry Up the Euphrates   *144*
    17:3, 12   "Tin Horn" Kings   *145*
    20:1–3   He Got Out of the Pit Without a Bottom?   *146*
    6:2, etc.   Revelation and the ERA   *147*

Postface   *149*

A Word from the Author

This is a volume of light verse. Although each of the poems was inspired by a passage or quotation from the New Testament, this is not a biblical study.

None of the poems in this volume is intended as a commentary on the passages quoted. To be precise, each poem has used the biblical text as a point of departure for nonbiblical humor.

Why the bible as a basis for humorous verse? To reiterate the words of Reinhold Niebuhr, cited in my first volume, *The Good Book Says* . . . , "Our greatest sin is to take ourselves too seriously. There is something fundamentally righteous and holy about our humor."

The sole aim of these poems, then, is the goal of all light verse. Their purpose is to amuse, to divert, to provide — in the words of Gilbert and Sullivan — "a source of innocent merriment."

— Ben Milder

The Good Book Also Says...

Preface

Doing the Lord's Work

As I'm pondering on the hereafter,
I feel certain that there will be laughter.
Since our funny bone is the Lord's doing,
It's a gift we should all be pursuing.

Other species are not so endowed.
Among beasts, we stand out in a crowd,
So the Lord's work you'll do, let's concede here,
When you laugh at the verses you read here.

The Gospels

Matthew 1:1–2, 6, 15–16

¹*The book of the genealogy of Jesus Christ,*
the son of David, the son of Abraham.
²*Abraham was the father of Isaac, . . .*

⁶*and Jesse the father of David the king.*
And David was the father of Solomon . . .

¹⁵*. . . and Matthan the father of Jacob,*
¹⁶*and Jacob the father of Joseph the husband of Mary,*
of whom Jesus was born, who is called Christ.

The Begats

When Joseph woke up, he was stunned
Because he found he had a son,
A baby lying there with not a lot on.
Joseph quickly was enthralled.
He said, "'Jesus,' you'll be called."
But who was Joseph? How was he begotten?

We learn that Judah was begat
By Jacob. Shortly after that,
Joseph's lengthy saga of begats began.
First, Perez — Judah begot him —
And from then on, seriatim,
More begats and more begottens, clan by clan.

In this same begetting fashion
Came Ram, Amminadab, Nahshon,
Then Salman, Boaz, Jesse — more, and yet,
Though not all those names are hallowed,
Each begat the one that followed
With a dozen more begats that I forget,

Then David begat Solomon,
Who begat, in turn, a lot of men
(Since polygamy was, in those days, permitted).
On and on, they just begat
From Asa to Jehosephat,
Then Manasseh, Amos, Azor — they all did it.

From one Jacob, thus it went
In direct line of descent,
To another Jacob. Who would think it possible?
But the Joseph Mary knew
Was begat by Jacob II.
You can read all those begats in Matthew's Gospel.

Matthew 2:1, 7–8, 13

*¹Now when Jesus was born in Bethlehem of Judea
in the days of Herod the king, . . .*

*⁷Then Herod summoned the wise men . . .
⁸. . . saying, ". . . bring me word,
that I too may come and worship him."*

*¹³. . . an angel of the Lord appeared to Joseph in a dream and said,
". . . flee to Egypt and remain there till I tell you;
for Herod is about to search for the child, to destroy him."*

Herod the Horrid

The Good Book says three wise men came to Herod bearing news
"A baby born in Bethlehem would be king of the Jews."
When Herod heard the wise men, he said: "We are not amused."

"Until now I have been supreme, the grand Pooh Bah, the greatest,
But if that rumor should be true, I'll surely lose my status.
Onto the royal ash heap, I'm afraid he'll relegate us."

And Herod, who was devious, opined: "I can't ignore him.
It looks like, when the chips are down, it's gonna be me or him
I'd better grab that child before the entire world adores him."

Then an angel of the Lord appeared to Joseph and his brood
And said: "It looks to me like Herod's in a nasty mood.
He seems to have gone 'round the bend; he's totally unglued."

And the Good Book's pages tell of the dilemma Joseph faced.
The angel gave Joe this advice: "Get out of town posthaste.
Head south until you see the Sphinx, because you're being chased."

Off they stole, in dead of night, in order to endure.
With seraphim to point the way, it was a sinecure —
The first recorded case of an Egyptian guided tour!

Matthew 3:4

4. . . and his food was locusts and wild honey.

They Must Be Finger-Lickin' Good

Matthew, though he makes no claim to being a physician,
Here, steps into the role of John the Baptist's dietitian.
He speaks of locusts mixed with honey as the total diet.
Though there were no complaints from John, I'm not sure I would try it.

That fare may well find favor with a person of John's piety,
But locusts and wild honey seem a bit short on variety.
So I called on my nutritionist and asked her just one question:
"Would such a diet tend to give a person indigestion?"

She said: "With carbohydrates it is laden, to a fault;
The same for protein, but it's low on fat as well as salt.
With honey it is tasty; it has calories galore.
But you won't locate locusts in your local health-food store.

Still, diets made of locusts and wild honey must be viable
Because they were John's sustenance — it says so in the Biable.

Matthew 4:3–4

³"... *command these stones to become loaves of bread."*
⁴*But he answered, "It is written, 'Man shall not live by bread alone, ...'"*

A Piece of Cake

The Good Book, in Matthew, says Jesus was tested.
 Said the devil: "Make bread from that stone."
But Jesus was not taken in. He suggested
That bread's not exactly a sine qua non.

"Satan, c'mon! Are you trying to tease us?
Turn stone into bread? That's a cinch — piece of cake!
I could do it with one hand behind me," said Jesus.
"David Copperfield does that one! Gimme a break!"

But in my house, my wife — Julia Child, she is not —
Performs miracles not so well known:
Using yeast and some flour and God only knows what,
She has often turned bread into stone!

Matthew 4:23-24

*²³And he went about all Galilee, teaching in their synagogues
and preaching the gospel of the kingdom
and healing every disease and every infirmity among the people.
²⁴. . . and they brought him all the sick, those afflicted . . .*

No Appointment Needed

The Good Book says that Jesus was a general practitioner.
He took on ills afflicting every indisposed parishioner.
He had no doctor's license, yet without a healing permit he
Cured every sort of sickness and unusual infirmity.

He cured the epileptics, both the grand mal and petit,
Leukopenia, ichthyosis, allergy to wheat,
German measles, sleeping sickness, also hepatitis,
Hypertension, nervous breakdowns, and appendicitis,

Torticollis, dengue fever, likewise psittacosis,
As well as some diseases that defy a diagnosis.
The miracles that he performed were wondrous to behold —

But nowhere does the Good Book say he cured the common cold!

Matthew 5:5

[5] *"Blessed are the meek, for they shall inherit the earth. . . ."*

No Closing Costs

Great lessons surface, some unique,
In the Good Book's Book of Matthew.
If you're among the mild and meek
And follow the right path, you

Are sure to be rewarded.
You are now a big landowner
All clear and free of taxes, 'cause
The Good Lord was the donor.

Although you'll be much richer than
The Emir of Kuwait,
It won't be things like oil wells;
It'll just be real estate,

And you'll inherit headaches
That you never had before:
Zoning problems, flood control,
Forest fires, and more.

You now own all of mother earth,
With its headaches and its chaos.
We're lucky that we're not so meek —
We wouldn't take it if you pay us.

Matthew 5:28

[28] "... But I say to you that every one who looks at a woman lustfully has already committed adultery with her in his heart. ..."

Let Thy Lust Rust

When you see a shapely bust
And your heart begins to lust,
There isn't much your mind can do about it.
Lustful thoughts like those are errant,
And you know, deep down, you daren't.
Although you think you've banished them, I doubt it.

If a girl with luscious figure
Makes your hormones pull their trigger,
The Good Book says, quite clearly, you'll repent it.
Nonetheless, if she's appealing
And you find that you're unfeeling,
You must be blind, infirm, or else demented.

Take the case of Jimmy Carter:
You'd have thought that he was smarter —
A president, most surely not a criminal.
On a pedestal we placed him,
But lusting in his heart disgraced him.
Now, that's adultery — although subliminal!

Matthew 6:3–4

*³". . . do not let your left hand know what your right hand is doing,
⁴so that your alms may be in secret; . . ."*

A Code of Alms

If you have wealth and on the poor you're likely to bestow it,
It probably is not good form to let the whole world know it.
So the Good Book says the left hand should be totally unknowing
Of what the right is doing, but let's look at the foregoing:

Just think of all the trouble that could possibly be brewing
If one hand should be out of touch with what the other's doing.
A violinist, for example, gets a screeching sound
If, when the right hand's bowing, the left hand cannot be found.

And think of poison ivy. If the left, alone, should catch it,
Suppose it itches like the devil, would the right hand scratch it?
So the Good Book recommends to those whose deeds are philanthropic,
It probably is wise to keep your mouth shut on this topic.

The penalties for bragging are both menacing and ominous,
But it wouldn't hurt to let folks know how much you gave, anonymous.

Matthew 7:15

¹⁵ *"Beware of false prophets, who come to you in sheep's clothing but inwardly are ravenous wolves. . . ."*

Would You Follow a Prophet Who Looks like Ewe?

False prophets, whom the Good Book says we should regard with loathing,
Are really in big trouble when they seek to wear sheep's clothing.
They think that their disguise will turn our thoughts in their direction,
But the holes that moths are drilling in that wool invite detection.

It is obvious false prophets need sartorial advice.
If they should opt for woolen clothing, they must pay the price.
They'll be unmasked by lepidopters and such mothlike varmints,
So instead of wool, they should try wearing polyester garments.

Matthew 13:57

⁵⁷... But Jesus said to them, "A prophet is not without honor except in his own country and in his own house."

... Except in His Own Country

If you would be a prophet with a passion for renown,
The best thing you could do would be to get right out of town.
You'd like your message to reach out to all in your vicinity,
But you are apt to wind up cloaked in total anonymity.

You look just like a prophet — sandals, white robe, and a beard —
But you must be six hundred miles away to be revered.
So the Good Book hints to prophets who set out to preach the gospel,
You'd better opt to preach as far away from home as possible.

Though fame and honors may await you in some distant city,
You dream that, back in your home village, you'll be sitting pretty.
They'll roll out the red carpet for you, but the nitty gritty
Is that the odds would be much better if you were Walter Mitty.

Matthew 14:6–8

*⁶. . . the daughter of Herodias danced before the company,
and pleased Herod,
⁷so that he promised with an oath to give her whatever she might ask.
⁸Prompted by her mother, she said,
"Give me the head of John the Baptist here on a platter."*

Odious Herodias

The girl said: "Uncle Herod,
You promised me one wish,
So give me John the Baptist's head
Delivered on a dish."

Said Herod: "That's so gruesome.
Don't you think that you might rue it?"
"Oh, no," said she, "it wasn't me.
My mother made me do it."

In all the Good Book's bloody tales,
There's none so mutilating,
And Herod soon went 'round the bend —
He began hallucinating.

He looked at Jesus: "I know you.
You're the one that I beheaded.
You're John, and you've come back to life!
I shoulda told that kid: 'Forget it!'"

It turns out Herod was a tool
For that vengeful witch Herodias.
I guess he wasn't very smart
To perform a deed so odious.

Matthew 14:17, 19, 21

¹⁷They said to him, "We have only five loaves here and two fish."

¹⁹. . . and blessed, and broke and gave the loaves to the disciples, and the disciples gave them to the crowds.

²¹And those who ate were about five thousand men, besides women and children.

Catering to the Masses

A housewife on a budget must possess creative zeal.
Adding water to the soup is one device.
If she's Jewish, she can stretch a meat loaf out with matzo meal.
And if she's Chinese, she can do the same with rice.

She can use the peel of oranges to embroider a dessert.
With bread crumbs, she makes stuffing for a turkey.
Although the crumbs are two weeks old, she says: "It couldn't hurt,"
And the beef stew from last year is now beef jerky.

When it comes to all leftovers, you can bet she's in there pitchin'.
For chicken soup, she uses chicken feet.
She works miracles each day within the four walls of her kitchen.
She's used one soupbone 'til it's obsolete.

But the Guiness Book of Records prize for stretching food for dinner
Goes to Jesus, who prepared a meal that fed
At least five thousand people, making him the clear-cut winner,
Using just two fishes and five loaves of bread.

Matthew 19:6

*⁶". . . What therefore God has joined together,
let no man put asunder."*

Tying the Marriage — Not

Before the minister intoned:
                        "Let no man put asunder,"
I should have had some second thoughts
                        And possibly have shunned her.
She's like the buccaneers of old,
                        Whose only goal was plunder.
I'm on the brink of destitution,
                        Struggling to fund her.
And now, besieged by all the bill
                        Collectors who have dunned her,
It finally has dawned on me,
                        Just like a clap of thunder,
That my banker has been saying:
                        "It looks like you're going under."
And now, to make things even worse,
                        She has become rotunder.

So when that clergyman intoned:
                        "Let no man put asunder"
And I agreed, could it have been
                        A monumental blunder?

                        I wonder!

Matthew 19:23

*²³. . . "Truly, I say to you,
it will be hard for a rich man to enter the kingdom of heaven. . . ."*

The Tithes That Bind

If on the list of heaven's hopefuls you would be enrolled,
You should be tithing regularly — so I have been told.
For centuries it's de rigueur for all churchgoing folk,
But you can't do much tithing if you happen to be broke.

If you are destitute, the gates of heaven open wide.
Apparently that's all you have to do to get inside.
Still, the Good Book says if you are rich, that's something of a stigma,
Which seems to be a riddle wrapped inside of an enigma.

If you're well-heeled, when your time comes, they close the pearly gates.
So if you want to enter heaven and don't want to wait,
Just spend as fast as you can spend and give away the rest.
When the IRS declares you're broke, you've passed the acid test.

And though you are reluctant to be parted from your wad,
Your money says: "In God We Trust," so put your trust in God.

Matthew 19:24

²⁴". . . it is easier for a camel to go through the eye of a needle than for a rich man to enter the kingdom of God."

Preposterous?

"A camel to pass through the eye of a needle?"
Why, the notion is simply preposterous.
The only thing sillier, you will concede, 'll
Be a hippo or rhinosterous.

Matthew 22:14

14"... For many are called, but few are chosen."

Where the Elite Meet to Eat

"Many are called, but few are chosen."
The Good Book's clear on that quotation,
But when you reach the supermarket,
There's more than one interpretation.

For instance, melons, when you've picked 'em —
Green or ripe or even frozen —
Hark back to the Bible's dictum:
Many are culled, but few are chosen.

Matthew 22:39

³⁹". . . You shall love your neighbor as yourself. . . ."

Love Thy Neighbor

    What Matthew here advises
    Could be fraught with dire surprises,
And that verse must come as something of a shock,
    For if I love myself, I find
    I must be similarly inclined
Toward every single neighbor on my block.

    Though those words could not be clearer,
    As I look into the mirror
And my image beckons me, just like Narcissus,
    I can sense there's trouble brewing.
    Will that verse be my undoing
'Cause I shall have to love my neighbor's missus?

    What a sad dilemma this is!
    If I love my neighbor's missus —
For, after all, she is my neighbor too —
    I am sure I'd love her madly,
    Which, of course, she'd suffer gladly
But which her husband would be apt to misconstrue.

    To avoid the consequences,
    I shall have to mend some fences
If I pursue that chapter and that verse,
    'Cause if I don't come to my senses,
    The existing evidence is
That I'll end up with two broken legs — or worse!

Matthew 25:14, 16, 18, 25–27, 29

*14"... a man going on a journey called his servants
and entrusted to them his property; ...*

*16"... He who had received the five talents went at once
and traded with them; and he made five talents more.*

*18"... But he who had received the one talent,
went and dug in the ground and hid his master's money.*

*25"'... I was afraid ... and hid your talent in the ground....'
26"... But his master answered him, 'You wicked and slothful servant! ...
27Then you ought to have invested my money with the bankers, ...*

*29"'... For to everyone who has will more be given, ...
but from him who has not, even what he has will be taken away.'"*

Score: Bulls 5; Bears 0

There are financial verities this parable advances.
First off, with money you're investing, you must take some chances,
For money in a piggy bank or buried in the yard
Is apt to yield a less than satisfactory reward.

This lesson, more than any other, you should take to heart:
To put your dollars in a cookie jar just isn't smart.
If, timidly, you sock your funds away in that location,
It's likely to be eaten up by mice or by inflation.

The lesson from this parable would seem to be, on balance,
The Good Book is the guide to use in husbanding your talents,
And in no time, you're sure to find yourself in a position
To double your net worth without a brokerage commission.

Mark 2:16-17

[16] . . . *"Why does he eat with tax collectors and sinners?"*
[17]*And when Jesus heard it, he said to them,*
"Those who are well have no need of a physician,
but those who are sick; . . ."

Break Bread with the IRS?

Here Jesus eats with the IRS, to try to save their souls.
And that was not an easy task — but those were Jesus' goals.
His critics cried: "Why does he put himself in that position?"
But Jesus said: "These guys are sick, and I am their physician."

Jesus, as their doctor, dined to save their souls from hell,
But you, the Good Book says, won't need a doctor if you're well.
To question what the Good Book says is patently heretical,
But let's assume the following (which, of course, is hypothetical):

The idea sounds quite promising, if you're devoid of ills;
You'll save a lot of hard-earned money on your doctor bills.
Although good health's a blessing, it's a joy not unalloyed,
Because all doctors, saints preserve us, would be unemployed.

If the Good Book's words, as stated, are definitive and true,
You won't need a physician, but, oh, boy, will they need you!

Mark 3:9-10, 14-15

⁹And he told his disciples to have a boat ready for him
because of the crowd, lest they should crush him;
¹⁰for he had healed many, . . .

¹⁴And he appointed twelve, to be with him,
and to be sent out to preach
¹⁵and have authority to cast out demons: . . .

A Franchised Operation

When it came to healing people, Jesus was the best,
'Cause he could cure the illnesses of all those in distress.
Inundated by the crowds, who gave him little rest,
He was, to use an old cliché, a victim of success.

He chose twelve men to preach the word and cast out evil spirits.
To each of those disciples he entrusted that authority,
So all of them went on that mission, and from what I hear, it's
A fact that though they missed a few, they did cure the majority.

He evidently felt that twelve disciples would be ample
To spread the word of God in every town across the nation.
I guess that you could say it was the Good Book's first example
Of what is called, in business terms, a franchise operation.

Mark 5:25-27, 29

^{25}And there was a woman who had had a flow of blood . . .
^{26}and who had suffered much under many physicians,
and had spent all that she had, and was no better
but rather grew worse.
^{27}She had heard the reports about Jesus, . . . and touched his garment.

^{29}And immediately the hemorrhage ceased; . . .

Not Typed and Cross-Matched?

The Good Book's words are words that many doctors might deplore,
But since they're in the Bible, they are words we can't ignore.

A woman called on many doctors, seeking one to cure her,
But none could do the job, nor could they even reassure her.
There the luckless lady stood, in blood up to her ankles,
With no one typed and cross-matched for transfusion — and that rankles.

From the implication of these verses, it is safe to posit
That the woman went through doctors just like water through a faucet.
When she ran out of doctors, she faced up to the reality
That the medicines they proffered couldn't do much for her malady.

But worse than their ineptitude, in fact, more reprehensible,
Each one of those physicians said: "Our house calls are compensible.
You must pay your bill right now, before you kick the bucket."
So she gave them her last farthing — and would you believe, they took it!

Although her faith in her physicians was not unexpected,
In retrospect, that faith, it would appear, was misdirected.
The zeal that she had wasted on the medical profession
She should have used to pray for the Almighty's intercession.

All she had to do was touch the hem of Jesus' raiment —
Presto! She was cured. And what's more, no one asked for payment!
The misery that she went through was not the least bit funny.
If she were smart she could have saved herself both time and money.

The sole prescription proved to be a single dose of faith,
And we know that's how it happened because that's what the
    Good Book saith.

(Does that call to mind the image of M.D.'s today, by chance?
"Plus ça change, plus c'est le même chose," as they say in France.)

Mark 6:47-48

*⁴⁷And when evening came, the boat was out on the sea,
and he was alone on the land.
⁴⁸And he saw that they were distressed in rowing,
for the wind was against them.
And about the fourth watch of the night he came to them,
walking on the sea. . . .*

Walking on Water

These days, if you are frantic
To cross the wide Atlantic,
You need a steamship like the *Q.E. II*.
But the Good Book lends the notion
You can get across the ocean
Without a steamship, tugboat, or canoe.

When Moses was confronted
With more trouble than he wanted
(He was, you might say, "in a sea of troubles"),
He promptly raised his staff.
The waters parted, half and half,
And the Hebrew people raced through on the double.

Though the exploit was unheard of,
There's another we get word of:
At the Jordan, Joshua's entire clan was jammed up,
And as the Bible has made mention,
Through the Good Lord's intervention,
The Jordan River's flow was shortly dammed up.

And there are others on the menu
Where that river was the venue —
That's the stream Elijah parted with his cloak.
The prophet said: "No way I'm fordin'
That polluted River Jordan,"
And he cleft the waters with one single stroke.

Now, to get from shore to shore,
Parting waters is a chore.
There ought to be a simpler route to take,
And it seems that Jesus found it:
While the people watched, astounded,
He just walked upon the surface of the lake.

It is right there in the Gospel.
Apparently, it is possible
To walk on water, though it isn't easy.
Yet that strange sort of behavior
Perpetrated by the Savior
Was repeated by St. Francis of Assisi.

Unless you're born with two webbed feet,
What Francis did, you can't repeat.
Yet, today, the act's performed on inland seas.
If to such things you're attracted
Each of you can reenact it —
All you have to do is strap on water skis!

Mark 7:1-2

*¹Now when the Pharisees gathered together to him, . . .
²they saw that some of his disciples ate with hands defiled,
that is, unwashed.*

Look, Ma — No Hans

Kleiner Hans, just age four, a Berliner,
Didn't wash his hands prior to dinner.
    Said his Mom: "In this place,
    Before you say grace,
Better wash them, or you'll be a sinner."

Muttered Hans: "Every day the same sermon."
(When Hans muttered, he muttered in German.)
    "It's the same old routine:
    'If your hands aren't clean,
You'll ingest ten or twelve kinds of vermin.'"

Then said Hans, who was just four years old,
"I don't think you have reason to scold.
    It is not impropriety —
    I am just showing piety,
As, in the Good Book, we are told.

"It's unlikely that you'll misconstrue it.
The disciples, in Mark's verse, eschew it.
    Thus, I have their permission
    (In the King James edition),
So you see, Mom, that's why I don't do it."

Mark 7:32, 35

*³²And they brought to him a man who was deaf
and had an impediment in his speech;
and they besought him to lay his hand upon him.*

*³⁵And his ears were opened, his tongue was released,
and he spoke plainly.*

If I Could Just Heal the Deaf and Dumb

I wish I were like Jesus, who could heal the deaf and dumb.
I have a class of students thus afflicted.
I try to hammer facts into their heads until I'm numb.
They're my problem, and to date, I haven't licked it.

They're unresponsive, each of them, to anything I say,
And not a single word is comprehended,
But the miracle of Jesus is repeated every day
The minute that their classroom time has ended.

As soon as they are out of school, their hearing is acute;
Their voices quickly come back; they're outspoken.
Next morning, they return to class, and once again, they're mute.
When I call on them the silence is unbroken.

If I were like the Savior for no more than just one day,
I'd make a scholar out of every student.
They'd answer all the questions that I ask without delay
And sit there silent when they thought it prudent.

But that is just a daydream. It is still the same old class;
I'm not their savior — that's not where I'm headed —
Yet if, by some strange miracle, a few of them would pass,
I'd like to be the one who gets the credit.

Mark 11:15

[15]. . . And he entered the temple and began to drive out those who sold and those who bought in the temple, and he overturned the tables of the money-changers and the seats of those who sold pigeons; . . .

No Place for a Pigeon

If you read the Good Book, it's not news
There were sinners who flaunted taboos.
    Though Jesus deplored it,
    Some sellers ignored it
By peddling live fowl in the pews.

His disciples and he were incensed
Such behavior was not countenanced.
    It was such a disgrace
    That they trashed the whole place
Where the pigeons were being dispensed.

The deeds of those sinners were Stygian,
For the church is no place for a pigeon.
    It may look like a dove
    As it circles above,
But it really belongs in the kidgeon.

Luke 1:13, 31

*¹³". . . and your wife Elizabeth will bear you a son,
and you shall call his name John. . . ."*

*³¹". . . And behold, you will conceive in your womb and bear a son,
and you shall call his name Jesus. . . ."*

Christmas Is a Two-Day Holiday

I

It is spelled out in the book of Luke,
By whom this gospel's written,
How John and Jesus came to be
And just where Gabriel fit in.

Gabriel said, as he appeared
From his home in Paradise,
"Zechariah, you will have a son."
Wife Elizabeth said, "That's nice."

Zechariah stared in disbelief.
"We're both too old and doddering.
It's been long years since I last had
A fling at so-called 'fathering.'"

Said Gabe, "Although it looks to me
Like you're a doubting Thomas,
Relax! It'll be a son named John,
And that's my solemn promise."

II

The Lord said, "Gabe, you've got the knack.
Now repeat that same behavior.
A son for Mary, and he shall be,
For all mankind, the savior."

So the reason on 12/25
That we trim Christmas trees is
As far as we can calculate,
It's the natal day of Jesus,

A day of peace throughout the land,
And joy, of which the essence
Is the annual after-Christmas sale
And returning Christmas presents.

Luke 3:14

*[14]Soldiers also asked him, "And we, what shall we do?"
And he said to them, ". . . and be content with your wages."*

I Wish My Office Staff Would Reread Luke

Jesus told the soldiers to be happy with their wages.
Those words were sage advice, not a rebuke —
Words that have come down from every boss throughout the ages.
I wish my office staff would reread Luke.

If I could borrow from the Savior that same admonition
As I dispense each fortnightly remittance,
They'd hoist me to their shoulders and give thanks in recognition
Of what they once regarded as a pittance.

It seems, in reading Gospel, my employees are selective.
In Luke, they hurry right past 3:14.
My emotional appeal is consequently ineffective
Or they'd heed the teaching of the Nazarene.

To transfer those instructions from the Good Book to reality
And teach them to my staff is my objective.
At payday, all my words are laced with utmost cordiality,
But their reaction's always laced with foul invective.

~ *Moral* ~

If you should want your office staff to view you as their savior,
Just try a cost-of-living raise to alter their behavior.

Luke 5:3

³Getting into one of the boats, which was Simon's,
he asked him to put out a little from the land.
And he sat down and taught the people from the boat.

Ship-to-Shore Communication

Ships at sea use satellites to talk — that's really clever.
They can stay in touch with almost any port.
They think because it's high tech, that the idea's new. However,
In fact, it's really nothing of the sort.

When Jesus left the water's edge and entered Simon's boat,
He was greeted with a thunderous ovation.
He turned and spoke, and even though it wasn't as remote,
His message was a perfect illustration

Of "ship-to-shore communication."

Luke 5:4, 6–7

[4] . . . he said to Simon, ". . . let down your nets for a catch."

[6]And when they had done this, they enclosed a great shoal of fish; and as their nets were breaking,
[7]they beckoned to their partners in the other boat to come and help them.
And they came and filled both the boats, so that they began to sink.

This Is No Fish Story

If you're the sort who would enjoy
A real fish story — the real McCoy —
You'll find one here, as the words unfold
In the greatest story ever told.

There's one in Luke that gets my vote.
Here, Jesus gets into a boat
And says to Simon: "Cast your net
And fourteen tons of fish you'll get."

Today's fish stories can't compete
With the fish he laid at Simon's feet.
Although it's no exaggeration,
It boggles the imagination.

Gone are fishing tales like these
From Isaak Walton wanna-bes,
Gone the miracles that get
An overloaded fishing net.

So advice for you who cast a line:
Some fish stories are divine.
With tales like those, you dare not tinker.
Just buy them all — hook, line, and sinker!

Luke 5:36

*³⁶ . . . "No one tears a piece from a new garment
and puts it upon an old garment; . . ."*

When You Have Your Back to the Wall

It is clear, from this biblical prose,
A new patch shouldn't go on old clothes.
>But if you're facing with urgency
>Some sort of emergency,

The patch could end up where it shows.

Let's assume a scenario here:
You've been chosen the "Man of the Year."
>At the Ritz, you'll be feted.
>It's a day you've awaited.

You're relaxed; you have nothing to fear.

Then — the seat's torn when you put your pants on,
And you're late, so you must take a chance on
>Any patch, old or new,
>And, without further ado,

Grab the first thing that you get your hands on.

It's your only tuxedo that's wearable,
But those holes in the pants are unbearable,
>So you sew on each patch
>Even though they don't match —

As a matter of fact, they look terrible.

At the Ritz, praises gush forth in batches,
And you blush, murmur thanks, but the catch is
>You must rise to your feet,
>Thus exposing your seat.

How do you finesse those new patches?

There is no need to fret or to panic —
It's not like you're on the *Titanic*.
>All you do is stand tall,
>With your back to the wall,

And your pants now become photogenic.

With the patches where no one will see 'em,
You have answered the call, *carpe diem*.
>What a clever device!
>The pants look kinda nice!

Still, they ought to be in a museum.

Luke 6:26

[26] "Woe to you, when all men speak well of you, for so their fathers did to the false prophets. . . ."

Every Sycophantic Antic

When they praise you to your face,
You should be on guard, in case
As words of praise they may not be intended,
For when you turn your back,
You could find yourself attacked
With prose your mother could not have invented.

If you're among the wise,
When they praise you to the skies
It wouldn't hurt to wonder why they do it,
For each sycophantic antic
They employ could make you frantic,
So you ought to take a further look into it.

They use words as sweet as honey,
And you prize them more than money.
You're blushing, and you find your pulse is racing,
But their words are false and corny.
And if you're falling for their blarney,
You'd better learn to be more self-effacing.

With some friends, you're on the spot.
One time it's praise; one time it's not.
Friends like these, you're better off replacing,
For there is no crime as heinous
As that of a two-faced Janus
Whose friendship hinges on which way you're facing.

Luke 6:27

²⁷". . . Love your enemies, do good to those who hate you, . . ."

Love Your Enemies

The Good Book here gets into sermonizing:
If you'll just love all enemies who hate you,
It promises a better fate awaits you,
Although that may seem just a bit surprising.
On Sunday, you should listen to your pastor.
Your enemies, he says, must be embraced.
Though the idea leaves a bitter aftertaste,
If you ignore his words, you court disaster.
I don't know where they came up with the notion
To love those who would love to cut your throat.
Since the logic seems increasingly remote,
It speaks well for your faith and your devotion.
The whole idea may seem to you bizarre,
But it's in the Book of Luke, so there you are!

Luke 6:29

[29] "... To him who strikes you on the cheek, offer the other also; ..."

Or Put Up Your Dukes?

To turn the other cheek is what the Books of Luke advises —
A noble thought which could be fraught with terrible surprises.
When you have turned the other cheek and find your jaw is broken,
The Good Book has some more advice that's equally outspoken.

Your primal instinct's apt to be an urge that's understandable:
To find the fiend and square accounts by fracturing each mandible.
If so, go right ahead 'cause in the Good Book it is written
"Eye for an eye, tooth for a tooth," so smite back when you're smitten.

A dilemma here confronts you: should you now put up your dukes?
Are some lessons in the Bible superseded now by Luke's?
Must you turn the other cheek when you are set on by some villain?
Although the Bible says so, I'm not sure that I'd be willin'.

Luke 6:31

³¹ ". . . And as you wish that men would do to you, do so to them. . . ."

Those Things That I'd Do unto Others

The Good Book says do unto others
What they'd do unto you.
Since that advice sounds flawless,
That is what I plan to do:

I plan to help them find their way
Whenever they are lost.
I'll seek out stores where they can buy
All merchandise at cost.

Whenever they are strapped for funds,
I'll give them an advance.
They'll all be guests in my château
(At discount rates) in France.

I'll stand by them through thick and thin
Whenever they're at fault,
Though I may take their protestations
With a grain of salt,

And when they're caught red-handed
And the jail doors open wide,
I'll bake each one a fruitcake
With a file concealed inside

And yet, one nagging question piques
My curiosity:
Those things that I'd do unto them,
Would they do unto me?

Since the Good Book's verse, however,
Gives no written guarantee,

I think I'll wait and see.

Luke 6:37

37"Judge not, and you will not be judged; . . ."

Judge and Jury

Jurisprudence doesn't signify that every juror's prudent.
Jurisdiction isn't how they verbalize.
A jury box is not a carton used to mail a juror —
And petit jurors aren't Lilliputian size.

A thing that's "jury-rigged" is not a jury setting sail,
And a judgeship's not a dinghy in disguise.
When a jury's hung, it doesn't mean that murder's been committed,
And "blue-ribbon" juries haven't won first prize.

It seems that Noah Webster is apparently at odds
With the Bible, though his words are clearly wrought:
His dictionary says the judge is one who should be judging. . . .
Still, the Good Book clearly says that one should not!

Luke 10:8

*⁸". . . Whenever you enter a town and they receive you,
eat what is set before you; . . ."*

Please, Sir, May I Have Some More?

    This is not an Aesop's fable.
    When you sit down at the table,
The Good Book says to eat what's served at meals.
    When the food is unappealing,
    You must hide what you are feeling,
Although, at the very thought, your blood congeals.

    While your stomach may be churning
    And for TUMS you may be yearning
And you hope that there's a doctor in the house,
    When the food is so disgusting,
    The Bible's words you must be trusting,
So shut up and eat your victuals and don't grouse.

    To clean one's plate, you don't debate,
    Although the food thereon you hate.
That's a gesture like a no-charge call to Heaven,
    But if you should turn your nose up
    Or you're the first who throws up,
Perhaps, instead, you should call 911!

Luke 10:23

[23] . . . *"Blessed are the eyes which see what you see! . . ."*

A Spectacle Dialectical

I said: "Dear ophthalmologist,
My vision's getting blurry."
Said he: "You're only one year late.
Sit in that chair. . . . Don't worry."

About an hour later,
He patted me on the shoulder:
"There's really nothing wrong with you
Except you're getting older.

"Millions would get on their knees
And say a prayer or two
If they could see what your eyes see
About half as well as you,

"So instead of buying glasses,
Here's the treatment that I'm urgin':
Put on your coat, go out and buy
A Bible, any version,

"Then turn to Luke, in chapter ten,
And repeat along with me:
'Blessed are the eyes, the eyes
Which see what you can see.'

"You're free of any eye disease,
So take Luke's verse to heart,

And don't forget to stop
At the cashier when you depart."

Luke 11:9

*⁹". . . And I tell you, Ask, and it will be given you;
seek, and you will find; . . ."*

Seek and Ye Shall Find

The Good Book's verse, here quoted,
Is immensely reassuring
That everything you've ever lost,
In time, you'll be securing.

But a task so overwhelming
Is just boggling to the mind,
For I have lost things it would take
Ten centuries to find:

> A canceled check that's in dispute,
> A cuff link on the floor,
> My list of things to do today,
> The key to my front door.

> I've lost my watch, my glasses,
> And directions to a party,
> Ability to read fine print
> (That's 'cause I'm over forty).

> I lose one sock from each new pair
> That I put in the laundry,
> And all the money lost in stocks
> Now has me in a quandary.

> I lost my firm deposit
> On a Caribbean cruise.
> I lost the crossword-puzzle section
> In the *Daily News*.

> I've lost each wrangle when I tangle
> With my loving mate,
> And now I've started losing hair
> At an alarming rate!

> And there are other things I've lost
> That are more aggravating —
> I even lose my train of thought
> When I am meditating.

In fact, I have so long a list
Of things I cannot find,
I'll probably soon add one more —
I think I'll lose my mind!

Luke 12:3

³". . . *Whatever you have said in the dark shall be heard in the light,
and what you have whispered in private rooms
shall be proclaimed upon the housetops. . . .*"

Wherein It Is Revealed That Lips Are Never Sealed

One conclusion we arrive at
Is that gossip's never private.
It says so right here in the Good Book's pages,
And those notions still persist,
With a somewhat different twist —
The Bible's words have come down through the ages.

The most innocent remark,
If it's whispered in the dark,
Is the sort of grist that feeds the tabloids' mill,
To which they all administer
A spin that is quite sinister,
Which then brings beaucoup bucks into the till.

With the media's crescendo
Of sex, dirt, and innuendo,
They think they've tapped a brand-new gossip craze,
But the Bible, years before it,
Took great pains to underscore it:
The Good Book surely works in wondrous ways!

Luke 12:37

*37". . . Blessed are the servants
whom the master finds awake when he comes; . . ."*

Be Sure It's Not Decaffeinated

The Book of Luke provides advice to put things in perspective,
If climbing up the ladder of success is your objective.
You do not have to be a rocket scientist to reach
The firm conclusion that, asleep, that ladder's out of reach.
If you forego siestas, Luke suggests that you'll be blessed
By both the Good Lord and your boss, whom you will have impressed.

But if, while at your desk, you have the urge to grab some z's, you
Should be quite sure the boss is not among the first who sees you.
A cup of coffee at your desk will tell him you're alert,
And hinting that it's not decaffeinated wouldn't hurt.

Better yet, if for that ladder's top rung you're still hopin',
A good idea would be to learn to sleep with one eye open!

Luke 13:30

*30"... And behold, some are last who will be first,
and some are first who will be last."*

The Human Race

Mr. A is punctual;
He's never, never late.
At bus stops, he's ahead of time
And doesn't mind the wait.

He's captain of the waiting line.
He radiates good cheer.
He's first to leap aboard the bus
And marches to the rear.

> Now, Mr. B is always late
> And always been that way,
> Dashing madly for the bus —
> The same thing every day.

> Coattails flapping, off he sprints,
> He's flying through the air;
> He's through the bus door as it closes
> On his derriere.

> Of course, A's seated in the rear,
> Where he's been before,
> While B stands poised beside the driver,
> Just inside the door.

> Every day the same tableau:
> A's calm as he can be,
> Then, at their destination,
> The first one out is B.

Somehow, it doesn't seem quite fair
That B should precede A,
But Luke, in chapter thirteen,
Has put it just that way.

It should not have to be like that.
With common sense, there's hope in it.
There's also a rear-exit door.
Why doesn't A just open it?

John 2:7–9

⁷Jesus said to them, "Fill the jars with water." . . .
⁸ . . . "Now draw some out, and take it to the steward of the feast."
⁹When the steward of the feast tasted the water now become wine, . . .

Turning Water to Wine

Said the father: "I remember — I ordered champagne
For this wedding of my only daughter,
And though I am normally loath to complain,
The wine that you served tastes like water.

"Whatever you've served — is it water or wine? —
It's apparent that it doesn't please us.
I'm not certain that stuff began life on a vine.
Just who do you think you are, Jesus?"

Said the maître d', "You chose the vintage and cru,
And it may come as a bit of a shock,
But the wine you're abusing — it's like water, that's true —
You chose that wine from your own stock.

"Though Jesus' wine miracle I can't repeat,
Your daughter is now thirty-nine,
And to marry her off is a miraculous feat —
Like the turning of water to wine."

John 3:8–9

*⁸". . . The wind blows where it wills, and you hear the sound of it,
but you do not know whence it comes or whither it goes; . . ."
⁹Nicodemus said to him, "How can this be?"*

Where the Wind Blows, CNN Knows

> The March winds doth blow,
> And we shall have snow,
> But when it stops blowing,
> Where does it go?

In Jesus' time, they didn't know which way the wind was blowing,
But today, on CNN, the weatherman appears all-knowing.
He isn't God, but he can tell the future and the past —
A miracle that would have left the three wise men aghast!

If only Jesus, in his day, had owned a TV set,
Just where the breezes go would've been info he could get.
Since data from the radar image he could not ignore,
I'm sure he would have opted for a different metaphor.

That knowledge, nowadays, is merely meteorological.
When Jesus spoke, his metaphor was strictly pedagogical.
The wind was merely Jesus' metaphorical invention,
Which he employed to capture Nicodemus's attention.

So when speaking of the wind's caprice, the Good Book makes it clear, it
Is just the Savior's metaphor for one born of the spirit.

> Just whence the wind comes from
> And whither it goes
> It seems they omit
> In the Good Book, op. cit.

John 7:14–15

*14. . . Jesus went up into the Temple and taught.
15The Jews marveled at it, saying,
"How is it that this man has learning, when he has never studied?"*

Better Late Than Never

I was a couch potato through my adolescent years.
My record for school absences still stands.
The thought of books and studying would fill my eyes with tears,
And college never entered in my plans.

You see, the Good Book said that Jesus didn't go to school;
It seems he got his wisdom from on High.
No classes and no homework — now, that really sounded cool.
I thought, if he could do it, so could I.

I thought by watching television, I was being taught
All the knowledge that one needs to know — and yet
Quite suddenly I realized that Jesus knew a lot,
And he didn't even own a TV set.

It dawned on me at last, I'd better opt for graduation.
The depths of Jesus' wisdom, who can see?
Instead, I used his wisdom as a source of inspiration,
And I graduated — at age forty-three.

John 11:17, 39, 43–44

*[17]Now when Jesus came, he found that Lazarus
had already been in the tomb four days.*

*[39] . . . Martha, the sister of the dead man, said to him,
"Lord, by this time there will be an odor,
for he has been dead four days."*

*[43] . . . he cried out with a loud voice, "Lazarus, come out."
[44]The dead man came out, his hands and feet bound with bandages,
and his face wrapped with a cloth.
Jesus said to them, "Unbind him, and let him go."*

Lazarus, Come Out

The Good Book says —
And each of us accepts the Good Book's word —
That Lazarus was ailing,
Passed away, and was interred.

Since he was not embalmed,
Nor did they give the corpse a shave,
They bandaged him from head to toe
And placed him in a cave.

His sisters said:
"When Jesus comes, of course we shall expect him
To do his best for Lazarus —
In short, to resurrect him."

And Jesus said: "Take comfort now.
Enough of all this weeping.
You may have thought that he was dead,
But he was only sleeping."

Of course, with Jesus,
"Sleeping" was his way of metaphoring,
But the people cried: "He's dead.
If he were sleeping, he'd be snoring."

"He's in that cave four days," said Jesus,
"But he's not forgotten"
Still, the people cried: "Don't open it,
Because by now he's rotten."

Jesus then replied:
"A good man's tomb is not his prison."
And when at last the tomb was opened,
Lazarus had risen.

Unbandaged, it was clear that
Back to life he'd been transmuted,
And even more miraculous,
The air was not polluted.

Then Lazarus said:
"Thank you, Jesus, but there is no doubt,
Those four days in the tomb
Are days I could have done without."

~ *Moral:* You're No Lazarus ~

If, when you think of Lazarus,
You think it would be nice
To pay a visit to your buddies
After your demise,

Forget it!

If you should seek to come back
When you leave this planet
And you are lying six feet deep,
Beneath a slab of granite,

You may ascend to heaven or
Fry in the fires of hell,
But that will be your last address
As far as we can tell.

So relatives can rest assured,
When your corpse decomposes,
That they won't have to stand around
With clothespins on their noses.

And when they carve up your estate,
They'll revel in the fact
That you will not return and sue
Each one to get it back.

Acts of the Apostles

Acts 16–28, the travels of Paul

I Wish I'd Been Paul's Travel Agent

I wish I'd been Paul's travel agent back in Bible days.
I could have made a fortune in a dozen different ways.
If I had handled his safaris, I could have retired
And lived a life of leisure with the money I'd acquired.

For Paul had traveled over land, as well as to the islands
On seas that ranged from tranquil to the ultimate in violence.
He visited Jerusalem and Antioch and Cos,
Perga, Derba, Lystra, and Cilicia and Troas.

He went to Antipatria, I think, or some such place,
To Syria, Beroea, Miletus, and Samothrace,
To Neapolis, Corinth and to Paphos and Lyconia,
To Phrygia, Phoenicia and to Tyre and Macedonia.

In Acts of the Apostles, nowhere do we come to grips
Regarding all the fine points of Paul's plethora of trips,
For there seems to be a scarcity of documented facts
Regarding Paul's itinerary in the Book of Acts.

But his travels took him well past the Aegean's scattered isles,
So he must have logged an awful lot of frequent-flier miles.
But he made his way, at last, to Rome, avoiding all disaster —
So his Visa/Mastercard must have been issued by the Master.

Acts 1:26

²⁶And they cast lots for them, and the lot fell on Matthias; and he was enrolled with the eleven apostles.

The Roll of the Dice

In the Good Book's Book of Acts,
We're presented with this fact:
They were minus one apostle, by attrition.
After Judas had defected,
The eleven left elected
To restore an even dozen as their mission.

Now, the problem was colossal:
They must choose a twelfth apostle.
Two candidates appeared, and when they'd seen them,
The apostles said: "They're pious,
Both Barsabas and Matthias,
And sad to say, we just can't choose between them."

They were hoping for a sign
From the Source that is Divine,
But the Good Lord said: "This time, you call the shots."
Since the issue was in doubt,
They just said: "There's one way out.
Let's choose between the two by casting lots.

"That's supposed to be a sin,
But what about the spot we're in?
It isn't rigged; therefore it isn't wicked.
What's more, it must be fair
If it's in a house of prayer."
And Matthias came up with the winning ticket.

So when your church's funds are sagging
And the collection plate is lagging
And you fear that any gambling would be sinning,
Go ahead — you won't be cursed —
'Cause the apostles did it first.
And that's how bingo games had their beginning.

~ *Thought for the Day* ~

Though the ethics may elude us,
That's just how they replaced Judas.
Ends justified the methods, so to speak.
Since that time, that's what determines
We have bingo games, not sermons,
In a house of worship, usually once a week.

Acts 2:4

*⁴And they were all filled with the Holy Spirit
and began to speak in other tongues,
as the Spirit gave them utterance.*

Men Spoke in Tongues

The Good Book says men spoke in tongues
When they became ecstatic,
And the Good Lord understood them,
Though their speech was enigmatic.

Men speak in tongues as well, today,
Beyond all comprehension.
Just hail a taxi in New York
And then pay close attention.

Acts 2:16–17

[16]but this is what was spoken by the prophet Joel:
[17]'. . . and your young men shall see visions,
and your old men shall dream dreams; . . .'

Old Men Dream Dreams

In the visions of young men, the norm
Has to do with the feminine form.
    If those dreams reach fruition
    With the lady's permission,
That is really no cause for alarm.

And the Good Book says oldsters dream dreams
Very likely with similar themes.
    Though they're oftentimes glorious,
    Those dreams are notorious
For coming apart at the seams.

Acts 4:32, 5:1-2

*4:32... those who believed were of one heart and soul,
and no one said that any of the things which he possessed was his own,
but they had everything in common.*

*5:1But a man named Ananias
with his wife Sapphira sold a piece of property,
2and with his wife's knowledge he kept back some of the proceeds,
and brought only a part and laid it at the apostles' feet.*

Would a Real-Estate Salesman Lie to You?

Ananias was a liar, in the Good Book we are told.
He pocketed some profits from the property he sold.
This was, of course, a "no-no," since all holdings were communal,
And Peter said: "You're lying. I shall act as a tribunal."
He said: "The rules are very clear — when anyone diverts
A portion of his property, he'll get his just deserts."

Now, Peter wasn't joking, for he viewed with disapproval
All liars, and he wouldn't shed a tear at their removal.
That is just what happened — Ananias passed away.
They wrapped him in a shroud and buried him without delay.
The body was still warm, without a hint of rigor mortis.
That's how the body must have been, 'cause that's what the report is.

Now, wife Sapphira didn't know of Ananias' fate.
When she came home, she said: "Hi, dear. I'm sorry that I'm late."
But Peter said: "No hurry. Since you knew about the plot,
It's probable you'll meet your husband shortly, like as not."
And she, too, perished quickly and, as quickly, was interred.
It happened just like that. It's in the Good Book, word for word.

Today, you wouldn't act like Ananias inasmuch as
The IRS would very quickly have you in their clutches,
So remember Ananias' fate, reported here in Acts,
And yield with grace each penny that the IRS extracts.

Acts 5:3, 5:5, 9:17–18, 23:2

*5:3*But Peter said,
"Ananias, why has Satan filled your heart to lie . . . ?"

*5:5*When Ananias heard these words, he fell down and died. . . .

*9:17*So Ananias departed and entered the house.
And laying his hands on him he said,
"Brother Saul, the Lord Jesus . . . has sent me
that you may regain your sight . . ."
*18*And immediately something like scales fell from his eyes
and he regained his sight. . . .

*23:2*And the high priest Ananias commanded those who stood by him . . .

Down to Our Last Three Ananiases

The Good Book has no characters with names like Smith or Jones;
There are no Goldsteins, Rockefellers, Kellys, or Malones.
So in the Book of Acts, why did Luke choose to mystify us
By giving us three characters with one name, "Ananias"?

There was the Ananias who, it seems, had told a whopper
In chapter five, verse three, of Acts and quickly came a cropper,
Then, later on, another one whose given name's identical —
A whole new Ananias, although equally authentical.

And for the more angelic one, who gave Saul back his sight,
I'd make of him a hero and call him Mr. Light;
As for the other Ananias, since he is a cleric,
I'd name him something just as fitting, but more esoteric.

Though names like Dark and Light would make the text more exegetical,
To change three Ananiases would seem to be heretical
So if you throw your hands up and are drowning in confusion,
You're not the only one who must've come to that conclusion.

Acts 5:18-19

*¹⁸they arrested the apostles and put them in the common prison.
¹⁹But at night an angel of the Lord opened the prison doors
and brought them out . . .*

Absquatulate?

Suppose . . .

You're stuck in jail, and you can't make bail,
And your lawyer's efforts prove to be of no avail.
You'd like to leave, but there's no reprieve,
But you could still have aces hidden up your sleeve.

If you're loath to dwell in your barred cell,
Just do as the apostles did and say farewell.
Although confined and much maligned,
They were free, because an angel was the mastermind.

Don't be caught nappin'. When you hear wings flappin',
It may be that same angel who can makes things happen.
You will leave the place in a state of grace
And leave like the apostles did — without a trace.

We reiterate, don't hesitate —
Just use the wings of angels to absquatulate.

Acts 9:25

²⁵but his disciples took him by night and let him down over the wall, lowering him in a basket.

A Tisket, a Tasket, a Very Welcome Basket

The city of Damascus
Was surrounded by a wall,
And the Hebrew people in that city
Didn't take to Saul.

"Your sermons are unwelcome,
And your words we're disavowin'.
We thought that you were one of us,
But you have let us down."

Then Saul's disciples said: "Those Jews
Are about to blow a gasket,
And we are fearful for your life,
So we bought ourselves a basket.

"We've had a meeting, and we think
It's time to blow this town.
And though Damascus' walls are high,
We won't let you down."

That night they put Saul in the basket,
Clad in just his gown,
Placed the basket on the wall,
And gently let him down.

So the Good Book tells us in Acts, nine,
That when they let Saul down
(Although it sounds confusing),
They didn't let him down.

That's the gospel truth, if you should ask us;
That's what happened in Damascus.

Acts 11:4–6

⁴But Peter began and explained . . . :
⁵"I was in the city of Joppa praying;
and in a trance I saw a vision, something descending,
like a great sheet, let down from heaven by four corners;
and it came down to me.
⁶Looking at it closely I observed animals and beasts of prey
and reptiles and birds of the air. . . ."

No Fancy Linen on the Table?

When the Israelites were hungry in the desert, they had manna
Showered down in bulk by the Almighty — shout hosannah!
But that seemed awfully messy, and the Good Lord pondered whether
He ought to make things neater, so He got His act together.

If you will read the Acts of the Apostles, you will find
Some catering that's more like what the Good Lord had in mind.
When Peter said: "I'm hungry; what I eat is immaterial,"
A Voice came down from Heaven — or at least some place sidereal:

"This is the Good Lord speaking; I can manage what you ask.
Although We don't have Irish linen or things like damask,
You may rest assured that any food you get to eat
Will come to you from Heaven's kitchen on a clean white sheet."

And there you have the details of what Peter saw while praying
In Joppa, where, the Book of Acts informs us, he was staying.

Acts 12:21–23

²¹. . . Herod put on his royal robes, took his seat upon the throne,
and made an oration to them.
²²And the people shouted, "The voice of a god, and not of man!"
²³Immediately an angel of the Lord smote him,
because he did not give God the glory;
and he was eaten by worms and died.

Coming to Terms with Worms

In the Good Book, it's clear the Almighty abhorred
The notion that one man could think he's the Lord,
Which brings us directly to Herod's demise. . . .
For vanity, he paid the ultimate price.
In Acts, there's a verse where the Good Book affirms
That Herod was smitten, then eaten by worms.

Now the Bible has many exotic such gimmicks
For punishing evil, but none of them mimics
What happened to Herod, who should have ignored
The people of Tyre when they said: "He's the Lord."
In the Bible, it's obvious no one adored him
But he'd been eaten by worms! And what's more, antemortem!

Sooner or later, we all come to terms
With the fact that we, too, will be eaten by worms.
But for all true believers, that will have occurred
A very long time after they've been interred.
And since none of us thinks that he's God, it's no wonder
That the worms will go hungry till we're six feet under.

Acts 13:1, 15:22, 15:37

*13:1... there were prophets and teachers, Barnabas,
Simeon who was called Niger, ...*

15:22... They sent Judas called Barsabbas, ...

15:37And Barnabas wanted to take with them John called Mark.

Simeon Who Was Called Niger

Suppose you have reached that so-called "certain age"
When your memory's slightly askew
And the Book of Acts deals with some names you should know,
But instead of one name, there are two.

Barsabas is Justus, and Bar-Jesus, Elymas,
And there's Saul, who, of course, is named Paul,
And Simeon, the Bible says, should be called Niger,
And John's name was Mark. That's not all —

Tabitha, the Good Book says, should be called Dorcas
(Her name means "Gazelle," which sounds sweeter);
And Joseph was Barrabas; Agrippa was King,
And then there is Simon, called Peter.

If you can't remember which name changed to which,
You have plenty of company, too —
For they're the same people who open their Bibles
About once in ten years — just like you.

Acts 15:1, 13, 19

[1] *But some men came down from Judea and were teaching the brethren, "Unless you are circumcised according to the custom of Moses, you cannot be saved."*

[13] *. . . James replied, . . .*

[19] *". . . Therefore my judgment is that we should not trouble those of the Gentiles who turn to God, . . ."*

Maybe Something Less Surgical?

The Judeans, by custom, were forced to revamp
One part of their person, with scalpel and clamp.
They said to the Gentiles: "You should be apprised:
If you want to be saved, you must be circumcised."

But the Gentiles said: "Gosh, that sounds terribly drastic!
Why couldn't your rules be a bit more elastic"?
Despite what you're saying, it's perfectly clear to us
You're likely to tamper with something that's dear to us.

"Why can't we be saved with some rite that's liturgical
Instead of that custom, which sounds much too surgical?
Since we Gentiles have skeptics here in our dominion,
We thought we should ask for a second opinion."

At that point, James spoke up without hesitation:
"There's a much simpler way to achieve your salvation:
If you'll accept Jesus while being baptized,
You'll find that you won't have to be circumcised.

"Baptism involves just a simple immersion,
Which will be enough to complete your conversion."
So the Gentiles, it seems, were no longer disheartened
At the notion of having their foreskins foreshortened.

No need, now, to part with an item so precious
To them and their spouses as that bit of flesh is.
So the Good Book reports that they made the decision
That they would forego that one organ's revision.

In the end, they decided they wanted no part of it,
And that, you might say, is the long and the short of it.

Acts 19:19

*¹⁹And a number of those who practiced magic arts
brought their books together and burned them in the sight of all;
and they counted the value of them
and found it came to fifty thousand pieces of silver.*

The Magic Art of Turning Money to Ashes

There came to Paul exorcists, whose beliefs bound them
To drive out all demons wherever they found them.
Paul spoke of the afterlife and resurrection,
And the exorcists gave up their black-book collection.

Though they listened to Paul and became true believers,
They shortly wound up in the hands of receivers.
It came about thus: to pay homage to Paul,
They gave up their Satanic books. That's not all —

They also elected to mark the occasion
By burning those books in a grand conflagration;
Then they looked at the pyre and moaned: "We understand —
We just barbecued books that were worth fifty grand!"

For true bibliophiles, it's not as bad as it looks,
'Cause the Ecclesiast said there are too many books.

The Epistles

Romans 1:22-23

*[22]Claiming to be wise, they became fools,
[23]and exchanged the glory of the immortal God
for images resembling man or birds or animals or reptiles.*

Their Prayers Were for the Birds

In Paul's epistle to the Romans, he quite clearly states
Why prayers to birds and animals won't open Heaven's gates.
For you, there'll be no latchkey if the gods you opt to follow
Are gods in human form, such as Poseidon or Apollo.

Back in those days, each tribe and nation had a predilection
For gods of every sort, which they relied on for protection.
In Istanbul, in ancient times, their weather god was Sharma,
And the Zulus worshipped serpents, an essential to their karma.

In early North America, Algonquins worshiped hares,
And Zeus, the king of all the gods, was claimed by Greeks as theirs.
A god named Apis (he's a bull) was loved by the Egyptians.
And the list is almost endless — there are gods of all descriptions.

Though ancients thought their deities possessed some big-league clout,
All those gods and goddesses have long since faded out,
With one exception — Bacchus, he's the Roman god of wine,
And when you worship him, you know your worship is de vine.

Romans 1:26–27

*²⁶For this reason God gave them up to dishonorable passions.
Their women exchanged natural relations for unnatural,
²⁷and the men likewise gave up natural relations with women
and were consumed with passion for one another, . . .*

Keep Your Passion Old-Fashioned

The Good Book says because men worshiped animals and snakes
And other gods in human form that obviously were fakes,
The Good Lord gave them up to sex perversions so obscene
That they would never turn up on a television screen.

And Paul has taken pains in this epistle to expound on
The details of those acts that nowadays are strictly frowned on:
Women linked with women, all cavorting in the nude,
Men in carnal congress doing things we'd view as lewd.

Today, we read that science claims such actions are inherent.
They'd like to make us buy that notion, but, of course, we daren't.
If we should blame it on a gene that's ultramicroscopic,
Must science and the Bible be at odds about this topic?

Yet if it turns out, in the end, that these traits are genetic,
It's bound to give the readers of the Good Book quite a headic.

Romans 7:2

²Thus a married woman is bound by law to her husband as long as he lives; . . .

The Man of Her Dreams

When a man and his helpmeet trade screams,
Wedded bliss comes apart at the seams.
    The man she should cherish
    Makes each night nightmarish. . . .
In that sense, he's the man of her dreams

When she said "I do," she must have erred.
When he speaks, it's all four-letter words;
    Obscene words she can't brook,
    Words like "wash," "iron," and "cook" —
It's a theater of the absurd.

So to the marriage vows carefully listen —
It is not all just huggin' and kissin',
    And you'd better think twice
    Before the old shoes and rice.
After that, he is yours — and you're his'n.

Romans 10:11-12

*[11]The scripture says, "No one who believes in him will be put to shame."
[12]For there is no distinction between Jew and Greek;
the same Lord is Lord of all . . .*

Knishes and Spanokopita

Paul addressed both the Jew and the Grecian,
And he threw in, I'm sure, the Phoenician.
    To those masses, said Paul,
    "Come with me, one and all,
There is not one among you that we shun."

Said the Jews, in reply: "We're not Greeks.
Doesn't Paul know just whereof he speaks?"
    Cried the Greeks: "We're not Jews.
    We'd have too much to lose.
We're as different as valleys and peaks.

"We have spanokopita each meal,
While the Jews have knishes with veal.
    With the Jews we're at odds
    'Cause we have multiple gods,
Which, to them, seems to be a big deal."

Then said Paul, who was speaking for God:
"While the notion may seem, right now, odd,
    Though you're ethnically varied,
    When to Jesus you're married,
In his eyes, you're like peas in a pod."

Romans 10:15

[15] ...As it is written, "How beautiful are the feet
of those who preach good news!"

With My Feet for Locomotion

When I grow up, I think I'm gonna be a roving preacher.
I like the kind of life the preacher leads:
He walks from town to town to teach God's love for every creature,
And a pair of feet is all the preacher needs.

Chorus:
Oh, the preacher's life for me, the preacher's life for me.
I'm gonna be a preacher just as soon as I can be.
I wouldn't be the mayor, and I wouldn't go to sea,
Because the roving preacher's life is just the life for me.

How beautiful the feet of those who choose to preach the gospel.
I'd love to be the servant of the Lord,
But, of course, to see those feet, if I wore shoes, would be imposs'ble,
So calluses would be my sole reward.

Chorus:
Oh, the preacher's life for me, the preacher's life for me.
I'm gonna be a preacher just as soon as I can be.
I wouldn't live in palaces; I'd rather have those calluses.
Oh, the roving preacher's life is gonna be the life for me.

My feet will be a preacher's feet before I get much older.
I'll walk the land; my life will be complete.
And my pedal pulchritude will catch the eye of each beholder,
For to stare at them would not be indiscreet.

Chorus:
Oh, the preacher's life for me, the preacher's life for me.
The villagers will gather round, amazed at what they see.
They'll say: "Though you're not glamorous, your feet, somehow,
    enamor us."
Oh, the roving preacher's life is gonna be the life for me.

I'll be a roving preacher, with my feet for locomotion.
I'll show them off to everyone I meet.
I'll spurn all trucks and taxis as a sign of my devotion,
And I'll never stoop to hitchhike. I repeat:

Chorus:
Oh, the preacher's life for me, the preacher's life for me.
I'd like to bring God's word to every town that I can see,
'Til I get fallen arches from the many years of marches.
Oh, the roving preacher's life is gonna be the life for me.

Romans 11:18, 21

[18]do not boast over the branches. . . .
remember it is not you that support the root,
but the root that supports you.

[21]For if God did not spare the natural branches,
neither will he spare you.

Getting to the Root of the Matter

This parable involves a mighty oak tree and its branch.
Beside it stood a slender, quaking aspen.
The oak branch fell and landed near the aspen tree by chance
And left the slender, quaking aspen gaspin'.

The branch said: "As is evident, I've fallen from my tree.
If I just lie here, I shall soon be rotten.
What's more, within a century — or maybe two or three —
I shall be gone and totally forgotten.

Said the aspen, with compassion: "I appreciate your plight.
I'm pained to see just how low you have sunk.
It breaks my heart to see you, fallen from your lofty height.
Let me graft you to my slender, quaking trunk."

> The fallen branch looked quizzical:
> "To me, you don't look physical.
> How could a mighty branch like me survive?"
> The aspen simply smiled and said:
> "If you lie there, you'll soon be dead,
> But grafted to my trunk, you'll stay alive."

> "Though your grafting'd be meticulous,"
> Cried the oak, "I'd look ridiculous.
> For supporting such as me, you're not well suited."
> Replied the aspen: "Though I'm quakin',
> When I'm your roots, you're not forsaken.
> If you have faith, you'll soon be firmly rooted."

> Thought the oak branch: "To his credit,
> I kinda like the way he said it."
> But he's little. I don't know if I can trust him."
> "Will your slender trunk abort me?
> Do you think you can support me
> In the manner to which I've become accustomed?

"Where will I get my nourishment?
What I need is encouragement."
Said the aspen: "If you'll cling to me, you'll flourish,
And you'll have the ability
To live to oak senility.
The Lord will see to it that you don't perish,

"For He's behind the deal I'm makin',
So hop aboard and just start quakin'."

~ *One Story, Two Morals* ~

This fable has a moral, which is
If you get too big for your britches,
You're apt to fall — that fact is undisputed!
But the major lesson from this homily
Is that you won't be like that oak anomaly
If your faith in the Good Lord is deeply rooted.

Romans 13:1, 3–4

*[1]Let every person be subject to the governing authorities.
For there is no authority except from God, . . .*

*[3]. . . Then do what is good, and you will receive his approval,
[4]for he is God's servant for your good. . . .*

Go Right to the Top

Suppose that you've been speeding and they hale you into court,
And the judge, it's quite apparent, is a most unpleasant sort,
And the officer who flagged you down is not a friendly cop.
Don't waste your time in pleading with the judge — go to the top!

Plead your case before the judge's Boss — that's my opinion —
For the Good Book tells us that the judge is just the Good Lord's minion
And probably your plea before the Lord will carry weight
If you will promise that, from now on, you'll decelerate.

This homily is meant to let you know just Who's in power.
So your faith in God should help you orchestrate your miles per hour.

Romans 13:6

*6. . . you also pay taxes,
for the authorities are the ministers of God,
attending to this very thing.*

Let Us Kneel and Pay

When the tax men appear at your door
Though you've given, they say: "We want more,
    For we've had a few looks
    At your company's books,
And we'd like a few words on that score.

"There may be several things you've ignored,
But there's no need to fall on your sword.
    Though we want every cent,
    There's no cause to lament —
We're just doing the work of the Lord."

I Corinthians 6:18

*¹⁸Shun immorality.
Every other sin which a man commits is outside the body;
but the immoral man sins against his own body.*

After You've Eliminated All Those Sins That Are X-Rated

The Good Book's words expound upon
The fact that sin is frowned upon.
It pulls no punches leaving that impression.
    In Corinthians, we are advised
    All sinning is to be despised,
That all of us are guilty of transgression.

    In 6:18, for every sinner,
    Whether oldster or beginner,
It offers tips to keep you hale and hearty.
    It says your body is your palace,
    So if you're planning to do malice,
Just aim your malice at some other party.

        Shun prostitution, fornication,
        Rape, seduction, masturbation,
        Out-of-wedlock procreation,
        Every sex abomination.
        Shun cigarettes, inebriation,
        And bungee jumping on vacation.

    Such immoral sins are hideous,
    And the Good Book doesn't pity us,
If in such sordid sins we seek to wallow.
    And because such sins are worse'n
    Other sins that spare your person,
Just choose your sin from one of those that follow:

        Subtle forms of tax evasion,
        Yielding to phone sales persuasion,
        Using sick leave for vacation,
        Double-parking on occasion,
        And major scandals such as praisin'
        Pastrami subs with mayonnaise in.

So you should start eliminating
Immoral sins, those with X-rating.
In Corinthians, this chapter tells us why.
It views such sinning with disgust.
I guess that means if sin you must,
Be sure your sins fall on some other guy.

I Corinthians 7:4

*⁴For the wife does not rule over her own body,
but the husband does;
likewise the husband does not rule over his own body,
but the wife does.*

I'm a Vassal in My Castle

The Good Book says that, in each house, the husband is the king,
And he rules his spouse's body, a priori.
But the Good Book hasn't visited my castle.

My spouse had other notions when she got her wedding ring
Regarding both our roles in our love story.
Guess what! She's now the queen — and I'm her vassal.

I Corinthians 7:8–9

⁸To the unmarried and the widows . . . remain single . . .
⁹But if they cannot exercise self-control, they should marry.
For it is better to marry than to be aflame with passion.

But Can He Drive at Night?

"About men," said my widowed Aunt Em,
"There are more of us than there are them.
    Though I'm widowed and aging,
    My hormones are raging.
I could use an 'intended,' pro tem."

That's a problem right from the beginning —
The available list is fast thinning.
    Until now, you have tarried,
    But, Aunt Em, please get married.
To do less, the Good Book says, is sinning.

You are eighty, Aunt Em, and you're bright.
Here's a profile of your "Mr. Right":
    He's not sexy nor handsome
    Nor worth a king's ransom,
But at least he can still drive at night.

I Corinthians 7:36-38

*³⁶. . . if his passions are strong, and it has to be,
let him do as he wishes: let them marry — it is no sin.
³⁷But whoever is firmly established in his heart . . .
having his desire under control, . . . he will do well.
³⁸So that he who marries his betrothed does well;
and he who refrains from marriage will do better.*

You Could Stay Engaged Forever

If your actions are unseemly when you're wooing
And your bride-to-be's aware of what you're doing
    And she says: "OK, let's do it,"
    It is likely that you'll rue it.
A marriage is what you should be pursuing.

If your passion, though, is something you can smother
And your behavior is quite proper to each other,
    With that sort of an endeavor
    You could stay engaged forever.
In fact, you might as well have been her brother.

If that's carried to extremes, true love is thwarted,
But the Good Book says that course is well-regarded.
    Though we're all monotheistic,
    That still seems unrealistic,
And a Gallup poll's unlikely to support it.

I Corinthians 9:9

*⁹For it is written in the law of Moses,
"You shall not muzzle an ox when it is treading out the grain."* . . .

An Oxymoron

If an ox is on the job and
While it's treading down the grain
Does some gleaning,
That wouldn't seem to justify,
The Good Book makes it plain,
Intervening.

The matter of the muzzling
Of an ox evokes surprises;
It's quite puzzling.
How would the farmer, when you think
About most oxen sizes,
Do the muzzling?

Although it's hypothetical,
It's something that I've brooded
Heretofore on.
An ox that lets itself be so subdued
Must be, I have concluded,
An "oxymoron."

I Corinthians 12:14–15, 17

¹⁴For the body does not consist of one member but of many.
¹⁵If the foot should say,
"Because I am not a hand, I do not belong to the body,"
that would not make it any less a part of the body.

¹⁷If the whole body were an eye, where would be the hearing?
If the whole body were an ear, where would be the sense of smell?"

The Ankle Bone's Connected to the Shin Bone

The Good Book says each human is unique, a maze of pieces,
And no one piece is fully in control.
But there are some exceptions that could modify this thesis,
Where one piece seems to represent the whole.

That comes as no surprise to me —
For some are on my family tree:

>Uncle Al's compassionate;
>They say that he's "all heart."
>My cousin Bob can't drive a nail;
>He's "all thumbs" from the start.

>Aunt Esmerelda's profile's sharp;
>In portraits, she's "all nose."
>Cousin Joe's a gorgeous hunk,
>"All muscle," head to toes.

>Aunt Matilda's ever happy,
>"All smiles," so say her peers,
>And when it comes to hearing gossip,
>We know that Mom's "all ears."

If you assume they each possess one item so unique
That it's their entire body, you should know
That scientists insist some ninety-four percent of each
Consists of nothing more than H_2O!

I Corinthians 14:33–35

³³. . . As in all the churches of the saints,
³⁴the women should keep silence in the churches.
For they are not permitted to speak, but should be subordinate,
as even the law says.
³⁵If there is anything they desire to know,
let them ask their husbands at home. . . .

How Times Have Changed!

Women staying silent while at prayer?
    I can't conceive it.
Saying not one word while they are there?
    I don't believe it.

The Good Book's plea may well have been okay
    Back when Paul wrote it,
But I don't think that it would fly today
    As he is quoted.

Suppose I tell my loving wife: keep mum —
    Would she eschew it?
I'm certain that I'd never be so dumb —
    I'd live to rue it.

The message this epistle recommends
    Needs some revision.
It must because that's what my wife contends;
    That's her decision.

So we've reached a compromise: Make no mistake —
    From Paul it's quite a leap.
My wife's the one who talks when we're awake,
    And I talk in my sleep.

I Corinthians 16:1–2

¹. . . as I directed the churches of Galatia, so you also are to do.
². . . each of you is to put something aside and store it up, . . .

Ten, or Even More, Percent

In Corinthians, it's evident,
For the church to be benevolent,
It needed monies, which then went
For good works for the indigent.
So the Good Book set a precedent,
And today things are no different
From St. Paul's day, when the intent
Was to have you part with ten percent
Of hard-earned funds (which represent
Large sums, if you are affluent),

A part of which then would be spent
To erect some sort of monument
In stone or canvas or cement,
Of which the more magnificent
Remain as an embellishment
In churches on the continent,
To remind us where the money went.

II Corinthians 9:2–5

²... I boast about you to the people of Macedonia ...
³... our boasting about you may not prove vain ...
⁴lest if some Macedonians come with me
and find that you are not ready, ...
⁵So I thought it necessary
to urge the brethren to go on to you before me,
and arrange in advance for this gift you have promised,
so that it may be ready not as an exaction but as a willing gift.

Give Until It Hurts

Dear Corinthians, wrote Paul,
"I salute you, one and all.
I am coming, and I'll soon be at your gate.
Brother Titus will precede me,
And I'm sure that he won't need me.
His job will simply be to pass the plate.

To the mother church, give thanks
By breaking out your piggy banks,
And show your true Corinthian largesse
So that when I do come calling
There will be no caterwauling
Or pleading that you're really penniless.

If your cash is not forthcoming
(Though that thought is almost numbing),
The church cannot exist on prayer forever.
Please don't be more parsimonious
Than those poor old Macedonians,
Who'd love to show you up in this endeavor.

Of course, there's no true parity
When it comes to Christian charity,
So Titus' task need not be controversial,
And do not look askance
If he's collecting in advance
To free me from the crass and the commercial.

Farewell, brethren, live in peace,
And may your net worth soon increase
In a spirit that is almost halcyonian.
You will surely make my day
If I can kneel and pray
That you'll outdo the lowly Macedonians.

II Corinthians 9:7

*⁷Each must do as he has made up his mind,
not reluctantly or under compulsion, for God loves a cheerful giver.*

If You'd Be in God's Good Graces, Put a Smile upon Your Faces

If you'd be in God's good graces,
Put a smile upon your faces
When you give, 'cause that's the opposite of sinning.
When you're parting with large sums,
You must show off your teeth and gums
And give until it hurts — i.e., from grinning.

Let your face reflect good cheer
As you dig deep every year,
For the Good Lord loves a man who gives with flair.
He's not apt to misconstrue it
If you're laughing when you do it,
Though your accountants may be tearing out their hair.

And let me give you one small earful —
Though the Good Book says, "Be cheerful,"
It had better not be just a silly grin.
Though your gift may have appeal,
That smile had better be for real,
Because the Lord is not so easily taken in.

There's just one sine qua non —
It's a talent you must hone,
Which the Lord is said to view with approbation.
You must abandon the austere
And just grin from ear to ear —
And don't forget to make a large donation.

II Corinthians 10:10

*[10]For they say: "His letters are weighty and strong,
but his bodily presence is weak, and his speech is of no account."*

Paul Puts It in Writing

Corinthians seemed to be hostile
To the speeches of Paul the Apostle,
    But the same words in writing
    Became so inviting
That their zeal bordered on the colossal.

Whenever Paul preached to the locals,
They cried: "Though we don't own bifocals
    And we may have to squint,
    Please put it in print
And spare us your no-account vocals."

One last thought that I'd like to inject:
If St. Paul were alive, I expect
    It's unlikely he'd be
    On prime network TV
If what Corinthians says is correct.

II Corinthians 11:14–15

*[14]And no wonder,
for even Satan disguises himself as an angel of light.
[15]So it is not strange if his servants
also disguise themselves as servants of righteousness. . . .*

The Devil Wears Many Disguises

Here a biblical question arises:
If the devil wears many disguises,
    Should you waste time debatin'
    Which one's the real Satan,
To avoid some unwelcome surprises?

But my wife has no fears on that score —
She knows who Old Nick is. What's more,
    When I come home quite late
    In an inebriate state,
She is waiting for me at the door.

My clothes I've contrived to dishevel,
Mute evidence of the night's revel.
    As I stagger in, yawning,
    At three in the morning,
My wife moans: "You look like the devil."

II Corinthians 12:14

*[14] . . . for children ought not to lay up for their parents,
but parents for their children.*

Child Support

The Good Book says that children need not put by for their folks,
But there are certain questions that this platitude evokes.
Although we feel the Good Book is the ultimate authority,
Do parents keep on putting by when kids reach their majority?
The words of Paul are clearly meant to be a metaphor,
But just how far does child support continue? Furthermore,

    A dilemma here confronts us,
    For the in Good Book's verse, it wants us
To look at parents as the sole providers.
    They must put by for their heirs,
    I assume, in equal shares,
And it clearly disapproves of all backsliders.

    But in the Bible it is written:
    When, by old age, you are smitten
And your children then inherit your estate,
    Even if they're *compos mentis*,
    Who'll act *in loco parentis*
As soon as you have gone to meet your fate?

    While the Good Book here has shown us,
    In the words of Paul, the onus
Rests with the parents, what about those heirs?
    They are orphans, it is true,
    But the youngest's fifty-two!
Are they old enough to manage their affairs?

                I assume that, in a pinch,
                They could turn to Merrill-Lynch.

Ephesians 4:26

[26]... *do not let the sun go down on your anger,* ...

If You're Hotheaded, Cool It

The Good Book says that fits of pique should never be protracted.
They should be gone when day comes to a close,
Or from your list of bosom buddies, you will be subtracted
Unless you make yourself less bellicose.

If you're hotheaded, you must learn to be less disputatious
Before the sun sets somewhere in the west.
Your wisest course would be for you to try to be more gracious.
That's what the Bible says is for the best.

If you would give your wife a kiss and in your arms enfold her,
She'll know that your wild temper you've forsaken.
But if, at bedtime, you still have a chip upon your shoulder,
All you'll have are splinters when you waken.

So before the sun goes down, forget about your fits of pique.
You'll feel much better if your mind is set on it.
And you might venture, in due time, to turn the other cheek —
But, somehow, I don't think that I would bet on it.

Ephesians 5:13

¹³but when anything is exposed by the light it becomes visible, for anything that is visible is light.

Light Verse

There are laws the Good Book doesn't cite
Regarding the physics of light,
    And so this example
    Should be more than ample
To show it's not all black and white:

There's my neighbor, an absolute fright.
She is part of the neighborhood blight.
    She weighs 300 plus,
    So it makes sense to us
That she's visible, but she's not light!

Ephesians 6:5, 9

⁵Slaves, be obedient to those who are your earthly masters, . . .

⁹Masters, do the same to them, and forbear threatening, knowing that he who is both their Master and yours is in heaven, and that there is no partiality with him.

The CEO vs. the CIO

In this verse, there's sage advice: you should treat your workers nice,
For the Good Book says that they deserve equality
And for those who disobey, there will be a price to pay,
Unknown back in the days of biblicality.

At almost any hour, you could feel the unions' power
If workers' equal rights you choose to spurn.
And I'll share with you the lowdown — they could institute a slowdown
And put an awful dent in what you earn.

If you abuse a peon, there is one thing they agree on —
They've got the clout, and they will show no pity.
If you would finish up ahead, just do as the Good Book said.
If not, you'll face their grievances committee.

After almost endless sessions, you will have to make concessions
With a not entirely unexpected sequel,
So before a crisis comes up, give the Bible's message "thumbs up"
And begin to treat each worker as an equal,

And you'll be held to that accord
By both the unions and the Lord.

Colossians 2:16

*16Therefore let no one pass judgment on you
in questions of food and drink . . .*

Even When You Get a Bum Steer

All food critics seem to know
When the food is just so-so
Or the owner's cavalier
About his steaks, when it is clear
What you get is a bum steer.

Though the critics' words are valid
When they criticize the salad,
If they are at all astute,
Though their judgment is acute,
They must keep that judgment mute,

For the Good Book makes it plain
They're commanded to refrain,
No matter what they think,
From criticizing food and drink,
Or they'll be teetering on the brink.

As critics near their judgment day,
Both the chef and sommelier
Will rejoice, for, like as not,
Where critics end up, it's their lot
That the food is always hot!

Colossians 3:20-21

[20]*Children, obey your parents in everything,*
for this pleases the Lord.
[21]*Fathers, do not provoke your children,*
lest they become discouraged.

Spare the Rod? How Odd of God!

One day my teenage son and heir came racing through the door:
"I know you gave me my allowance, but I need some more.
I'm meeting my amigos, and the mall is where we're heading.
But I looked into my bank account, and all I have is red ink."
I'll need some folding money for the video machines,
And I hate to leave the house without a few bucks in my jeans."

> "Did you straighten up your room?
> Are your studies all complete?
> Did you empty the dishwasher?
> Did you feed the parakeet?
> Did you write to your grandparents?
> Did you carry out the trash?
> Unless you've finished every chore, forget about the cash.

> "You're just one member of this clan,
> So why must I remind you?
> Whenever there is work to do,
> The FBI can't find you."

"But, Father, in Colossians, the Good Book makes it plain:
From such draconian measures, you're commanded to refrain,
Because if you upbraid me and my sloth is your obsession,
You will end up paying all the bills for my depression."

But the Good Book also says it's true kids must obey each parent,
A point of view that kids eschew as patently aberrant.
So now there is a conflict in the generation gap,
And parents should not be allowed to fall into the trap.

The kids' behavior may leave parents thoroughly disgusted,
But the parents bear the onus if the kids are maladjusted.
So don't provoke your children, though at times it's hard to swallow it,
But that word comes from the Good Book, so I guess you'd better
    follow it.

I Thessalonians 4:10–11

[10] . . . we exhort you, brethren, . . .
[11] . . . to mind your own affairs, . . .

Things May Not Be Too Rosy If You're Nosy

The Good Book pleads that all of us should mind our own affairs,
Though it doesn't cite the risks if we do not.
But there is no denying that the folks who do the prying
Must somehow pay for all the woes they've wrought.

If their principal diversion is confined to being nosy
And to meddlesome behavior they're inclined,
They are bound in time to rue it, 'cause they're sure to overdo it,
And you all know just the folks we have in mind:

There's the one whose eyes are roving, as he passes by your desk,
For a surreptitious survey of your mail,
And there's the neighbor who is prone, when you're on the telephone,
To bend an ear for any small detail.

If you're like those Nosy Parkers, one fine day you'll pay the price.
If on being a buttinsky you are thriving,
If eavesdropping has you spellbound, you are certain to be
    hellbound —
And that goes for those who relish backseat driving.

I Thessalonians 5:15

*¹⁵See that none of you repays evil for evil,
but always seek to do good to one another and to all.*

Housecleaning

Though our house wasn't dirty last week,
A thief cleaned us out, so to speak.
    The Good Book says I should
    Repay evil with good.
    Must I now turn the opposite cheek?

I am puzzled. What's more, I'm distraught.
If the miscreant is somehow caught,
    Do I plead the judge free him,
    And do we guarantee him
To correct the mistakes he has wrought?

Would we say: "When you paid your last call
And you hurriedly left with your haul,
    You forgot, being nervous,
    Our best silver service,
So that's rightfully yours, after all?"

Could that verse's words be overzealous?
If the Good Book, here, seeks to compel us
    To repay evil with good,
    It should be understood
That's a package not easy to sell us.

I Timothy 2:11–12

[11]Let a woman learn in silence with all submissiveness.
[12]I permit no woman to teach or to have authority over men;
she is to keep silent.

The Silent Sex? Aw, C'mon!

Why is it men don't understand
That women have been in command
From the time one came from Adam's rib
Until these days of women's lib.

Since the Good Book tells us that your wife
Must maintain silence throughout her life
And be submissive to your will,
Paul's words I'd like to cling to. Still,

My wife now takes a different tack:
On most occasions, she talks back
Without (or sometimes with) permission,
Defying biblical tradition.

She tells me: "You'll be devastated,
But today those rules are antiquated.
That message, dear, that you adhere to,
I'm not inclined to lend an ear to.

"So if our marriage is to last,
You'd better mend your ways — and fast!
Just go and earn the daily bread,
And I will say what needs be said."

The Good Book may have been correct,
Back then when gals got no respect,
But now you're apt to come a cropper
If you still think that posture's proper.

Though Scripture we don't disavow,
Some are gender-neutral now!

I Timothy 4:4

⁴*For everything created by God is good, . . .*

Broccoli Is Good?

The Bible tells us everything the Good Lord made is good;
His works we tend to view with admiration.
But I am puzzled when it comes to certain types of food —
Could He have had a Hand in their creation?

Some people just can't stand the thought of eating Brussels sprouts,
And they turn their noses up when they see broccoli.
For other folks, the thought of bird's-nest soup creates some doubts,
Although they aren't forced to eat it, loccoli.

Eels from the Sargasso Sea are apt to make one sicken,
And the same for dandelions in salad vert
As well as all those restaurants that feature blackened chicken.
Then there's chocolate covered crickets for dessert.

The French, who are devout, delight in eating things like snails.
They're the Good Book's bons vivants, there is no question,
While other folk (this is no joke) eat blubber cut from whales,
And from what I hear, they don't get indigestion.

Some gourmets claim that foods like these are truly tantalizing
Although you're sickened at the very sight of them,
But take a taste, at least, because the Good Book is advising
The Lord's the chef, so you should take a bite of them.

I Timothy 5:23

*²³No longer drink only water, but use a little wine
for the sake of your stomach and your frequent ailments.*

Any Port in a Storm

Here, the Good Book lets us know
If you drink just H_2O,
Though it satisfies your thirst, you cannot trust it.
It has minerals like iron,
And this is what'll be transpirin':
In time your small intestine will've rusted.

If it's water from the well,
You'll be hearing your death knell,
'Cause down there, microorganisms lurk,
And water from the river
Could be harmful to your liver,
For that's where protozoans do their work.

Bottled water is one choice,
But it's too soon to rejoice.
It's sterilized, and yet it is worth noting
That even then, there is some peril —
Though you think the water's sterile
In that water, unseen germs could well be floating.

The Bible says that, hence,
It would seem to make good sense
To utilize the grape to wet your whistle.
So it comes as no surprise
That most doctors now advise
Exactly what Paul said in this epistle.

And they never give Paul credit,
Although he's the first who said it!

I Timothy 6:10

[10]*For the love of money is the root of all evils; . . .*

The Root of All Evils

If the Good Book says that love of money is the root of evil,
It must follow that the lack thereof is good,
But, nonetheless, the destitute, since they are not naive, will
Trade places with the wealthy if they could.

If, to be free from all wrongdoing, you must give away your stocks
And don the tattered garb of parsimony,
You might have second thoughts about this seeming paradox
And hang on to your suits made by Brioni.

If such radical behavior seems to be a mite too drastic
And folding money's evil, you can still resort to plastic.

Titus 2:6

⁶Likewise urge the younger men to control themselves.

When Your Hormones Are Aflame

The Good Book says your goal
Should be maintaining self-control,
Which isn't quite as easy as it sounds
When your endocrines are storming.
It should be to you a warning
To choose with utmost care your pleasure grounds.

When your sweetheart, getting bolder,
Puts her head upon your shoulder,
It's an invitation that's not unexpected,
But such brazen-faced behavior
Will not sit well with the Savior,
So you must be firm and, though it hurts, reject it.

Then you hurry home posthaste,
For there is no time to waste,
And throw yourself, headlong, into the shower.
In this way, restrain your passion
In a most effective fashion
And give testimony to the Good Book's power.

Hebrews 5:13-14

*¹³for every one who lives on milk
is unskilled in the word of righteousness, for he is a child.
¹⁴But solid food is for the mature,
for those who have their faculties trained by practice
to distinguish good from evil.*

Some Sour Notes About Milk

What the Good Book, here, has taught
Has most dairymen distraught,
For it holds that milk is only fit for kids,
Who must wait till they're maturer
To become both judge and juror
Of what is right and what the Lord forbids.

If you can masticate your food,
Does that guarantee that you'd
Find the road to righteousness without a map?
Do evil deeds torment you less
When you become edentulous
And are living on just liquid foods and pap?

Now McDonald's is perplexed
When they read this chapter's text —
Should they serve Big Macs to just the erudite?
If they do, you'll hear kids holler
From Key West to Walla Walla,
Which just goes to show that kids know wrong from right.

Hebrews 11:11-12

*[11]By faith Sarah herself received power to conceive,
even when she was past the age . . .
[12]Therefore from one man, and him as good as dead,
were born descendants . . .*

Faith? Viagra? Both?

    Although you're as good as dead,
    In the Good Book it is said
If you have faith, it can rejuvenate you.
    Just forget hormone injections;
    With true belief, you'll have erections,
And your wife will once again appreciate you.

    With your faith, you've got the knack,
    But when you venture in the sack
Just add to piety Viagra (oral).
    If you give it half a chance,
    You'll find your faith enhanced.
Since the FDA approves, it's not immoral.

    Although faith was unassailable,
    Had Viagra been available,
Of begetting there would not have been a dearth.
    With that philter in their hand,
    Males would be in great demand
And responsible for more good will on earth.

Hebrews 13:4

*⁴Let marriage be held in honor among all,
and let the marriage bed be undefiled; . . .*

The Marriage Bed

A great deal has been written and a lot more has been said
Of sanctity and honor in the so-called "marriage bed."
Be it rollaway or sleeping bag or even just a cot,
The Good Book lets us know just what it is and what it's not.

For a marriage to be consummated, first it must be lawful.
Omitting that one small detail we're prone to view as awful,
For what the Bible tells us here just cannot be ignored —
To live in sin is obviously much to be deplored.

If you would put the "holy" into holy matrimony,
Go get a marriage license and be sure it isn't phony.
Then, in the marriage bed, to lasting love you can surrender,
But the Bible says be sure that you're not both of the same gender.

Of course, there are those sinners who are out for fun and frolic,
And though the term the "marriage bed" is meant to be symbolic,
The Good Book makes it crystal clear it's attitude turns sour
If the bed is in a room that has been rented by the hour.

So no matter where the bed is and no matter what its shape,
The Good Book has a dictum from which there is no escape:
Forget the funning; that's a sin. Instead, take this advice:
Adopt the hallowed custom that involves old shoes and rice.

Hebrews 13:5

*[5]Keep your life free from love of money,
and be content with what you have; . . .*

Just Be Happy with Your Lot

When there's nothing in the pot,
Just be happy with your lot.
That is what the Bible urges in this verse.
Though misfortune may have found you,
If you'll take a look around you,
You'll find that things could be a great deal worse.

You should smile when you feel blue —
Philosophically, that's true.
But when the landlord calls and you are broke,
Though you beef about the plumbing,
If the rent is not forthcoming,
You will learn that being destitute's no joke.

What the Good Book says is true —
That if money you eschew,
It might just help to guarantee salvation,
But if in your bank account
There's no significant amount,
It's just as apt to guarantee starvation.

James 2:1–3

[1]My brethren, show no partiality . . .
[2]For if a man with gold rings and in fine clothing
comes into your assembly,
and a poor man in shabby clothing also comes in,
[3]and you pay attention to the one who wears the fine clothing
and say, "Have a seat here, please,"
while you say to the poor man "Stand there," or, "Sit at my feet,". . .

The Front-Row Pews

You're off to church, clad in your Sunday best,
Hand-tailored in the very latest style,
Displaying lots of medals on your chest.
Says the usher, as you saunter down the aisle:

"The pews down front we're saving for the poor.
We realize that on one such pew you'd planned,
But we'll find a seat for you back near the door.
It's that, my friend, or you will have to stand."

In James, that's how this little drama works,
But in real life, when you're in the house of prayer,
Those front-row pews are seen by some as "perks."
You'll find the biggest givers seated there.

When the poor man sits down front, it isn't funny
If the rich man's back there sitting on his money.

James 2:14

*[14]What does it profit, my brethren,
if a man says he has faith but has not works? . . .*

Grab a Hammer

    Here is what the Good Book saith:
      If you just exist on faith
And your faith, with good works, isn't intertwined,
      A priori, it must follow
      That your faith's no more than hollow
If you don't reach out to help the halt and blind.

      Do good works and help the poor,
      And you'll profit, that's for sure,
'Cause the Bible says that method's apropos.
      Though it says here that you'll profit,
      You can't make a living off it,
'Cause rewards are in the spirit, not the dough.

      For example, do your part
      And return your shopping cart
Before some shopper's knee is dislocated;
      With discount coupons, don't be greedy —
      Give the whole lot to the needy,
Especially the ones that are outdated.

      Although it lacks in glamour,
      Jimmy Carter took a hammer
And roamed the land in search of work to do.
      Had he been inclined to roam less,
      There would be a lot more homeless,
And if Jimmy could do good works, so can you.

      But don't forget to make communion
      With your local builders' union!

James 3:8

*⁸but no human being can tame the tongue —
a restless evil, full of deadly poison.*

For Every Poison, There Is an Antidote

The tongue, known for its noisiness, can also be quite poisonous —
That's how it is reported, here in James —
And when it is used to poison us, it wipes out all the joys in us.
It's a cruel and lethal tool, the Good Book claims.

When the tongue is double-dealing and you're apt to hit the ceiling
And you wish, somehow, it would be stricken dumb,
There's a method that's appealing, tailored to with whom you're dealing:
Hold his head in water till the tongue is mum.

To put gossiping to flight, you must not give up the fight,
'Cause evil tongues are busy all the time.
And it's perfectly all right if you tape the lips shut tight —
That's a case of "let the punishment fit the crime."

I Peter 3:1-2

*¹Likewise you wives, be submissive to your husbands,
so that some, though they do not obey the work,
may be won without a word by the behavior of their wives,
²when they see your reverent and chaste behavior.*

Be Submissive to Your Husbands?

    Peter says the ladies
    Must be on their best behavior
And be ever reverent as well as being chaste
    So that a message will be sent
    To wayward husbands to repent
And not be, by their errant ways, disgraced.

    But "submissive"? They submit
    That is asking quite a bit.
They're well-behaved and don't mind being chaste,
    But they want it understood
    That, in all likelihood,
They'll insist the word "submissive" be erased.

I Peter 3:7

⁷Likewise, you husbands, live considerately with your wives, bestowing honor on the woman as the weaker sex, . . .

That Was Then, This Is Now

    This passage has a sequel,
    For women are now equal.
That took about two thousand years to happen.
    In fact, in actuality,
    There is no true equality —
I guess the stronger sex has been caught nappin'.

    If you cast your lot with NOW,
    The Good Book's words you disavow.
For it says that women are the weaker gender.
    When I brought this up, my frau
    Said: "That was then, and this is now.
You're no longer king at home, just a pretender."

    That scenario isn't funny,
    Because she controls the money.
To tell the truth, at home I'm just a peon —
    That's a fact that I'm lamenting.
    And though the Good Book is dissenting,
It's one point I'm not about to disagree on.

I John 4:1

[1]... *for many false prophets have gone out into the world.*

Dial 1-800-2BSAVED

Long, long ago, there was a day
When it was commonplace, they say,
For prophets to use feet for locomotion,
And if their preaching was untrue,
It was heard by just a few —
No more than just a droplet in the ocean.

Preaching is big business now.
A larger furrow preachers plow
Upon the airwaves all across the nation.
If to the TV tube you're glued,
A few false prophets will intrude,
But they're no discount house to buy salvation.

If you sin, you can't repent
By giving them a single cent.
That's just an act that you are sure to rue.
But if redemption is your goal,
That's why you have remote control —
To make those prophets disappear from view.

I John 5:16–17

*¹⁶. . . There is sin which is mortal;
I do not say that one is to pray for that.
¹⁷All wrongdoing is sin, but there is sin which is not mortal.*

Not All Sinning Is the Same

Not all sinning is the same,
So if you want to play the game,
Just choose those sins for which you are most suited.
If you must be a transgressor
When choosing sins, just choose the lesser
Of those for which you could be executed.

If you knew which sins are mortal,
You would shun them like a plague
And opt for lesser sins, if you could choose them.
That seems to make good sense,
For the sinner who repents
Not only can enjoy them but reuse them.

Jude 16

[16]These are grumblers, malcontents, following their old passions, loudmouthed boasters, . . .

Loudmouthed Boasters, Turn to Jude

Loudmouthed boasters, who are crude,
   And surly malcontents should brood
On the Good Book's words in Jude,
   And I think that I'd include
All those noisy grumblers who'd
   Logically conclude
That their nasty attitude
May possibly preclude
Salvation's quietude.
However, if they're shrewd
And their actions they have rued
And they repent their turpitude
And behave like they're subdued,
Those are the villains who'd
Earn the Good Lord's lenitude.

And that's what I conclude
From Jude.

Revelation

Revelation 1:10-11

*¹⁰I was in the Spirit on the Lord's day,
and I heard behind me a loud voice like a trumpet
¹¹saying, "Write what you see in a book
and send it to the seven churches, . . ."*

Put It in Writing

The Good Book says John's visions came in multiples of seven.
In the Book of Revelation, that same number is repeated:
There are seven churches, seven kings and angels straight from heaven,
And don't forget the seven-headed beast that was defeated.

A great voice like a trumpet's sound now spoke to John and said:
"My orders are: Write down in great detail your every vision.
Omit no jot nor tittle of the things you see. Instead,
Be sure that you record each episode with great precision."

There were so many sevens, just how did John keep them straight?
I guess it took a miracle to keep them all in order.
It may be idle thinking, but I'm moved to speculate:
Would there be still more sevens if he'd had a tape recorder?

Revelation 6:7–8

*⁷When he opened the fourth seal,
I heard the voice of the fourth living creature say, "Come!"
⁸And I saw, and behold, a pale horse,
and its rider's name was Death, . . .*

Behold, a Pale Horse

In Revelation, one passage that should be remarked on
Involves the four horsemen and what they're embarked on.
From the words of the text, there can be no mistaking
That they're up to no good — their aims are earthshaking.
The havoc they'll wreak is beyond calculation,
And the fate of the fallen is certain damnation.

If, behold, a pale horse should appear on the scene,
It's apparent at once that not all is serene.
Common sense ought to tell you that if there's a dearth
Of good deeds you should have performed here on earth,
It's too little, too late, for the time has passed when
You could wipe the slate clean and start over again.

If you're planning, somehow, to speed up your repentance
And, at the last minute, ensure your ascendance,
Forget it! Our planet as you've come to know it
Will go up in smoke, and you could end up below it.
In the Lord's Book of Life, let's just pray you'll be signed up
'Cause you'll be there forever, wherever you wind up.

Revelation 8:2, 8:7, 9:1, 9:3

*8:2Then I saw the seven angels who stand before God,
and seven trumpets were given to them.*

*8:7The first angel blew his trumpet,
and there followed hail and fire, mixed with blood, . . .*

9:1And the fifth angel blew his trumpet, . . .

9:3Then from the smoke came locusts on the earth, . . .

Not Even Louie Armstrong Ever Blew His Horn So Hard

The Good Lord said to Joshua: "Please keep this confidential —
For Jericho to fall, you're gonna need a small brass band.
Just seven trumpet players with fortissimo potential
Will wreck the walls of Jericho, exactly as I've planned."

If that strikes you as impressive, it was just a practice run,
A warmup for the prophecies you'll find in Revelation,
Which tells of seven angels blowing trumpets, one by one,
To let us know our planet's on the brink of devastation.

Each angel has a mission with the trumpet that he's bearing:
To wreak the Good Lord's vengeance on transgressors, every one.
There is no evil on this earth those trumpets will be sparing —
All types of living things will come to grief before He's done.

In his vision, John saw plagues the Good Book says the Lord will send us.
There was hail and fire and other woes that cannot be ignored,
Like giant locusts from the pit, unshackled to torment us,
So that with each trumpet blast, you'll feel the full wrath of the Lord.

If you've paid close attention, then it ought to be apparent
That not even Louie Armstrong ever blew his horn so hard.
So you'd better mend your ways — because they probably were errant —
Before you hear those trumpets of the angels of the Lord.

Revelation 13:1–2

*¹And I saw a beast rising out of the sea,
with ten horns and seven heads, with ten diadems upon its horns
and a blasphemous name upon its heads.
²And the beast that I saw was like a leopard,
its feet were like a bear's, and its mouth was like a lion's mouth.
And to it the dragon gave his power and his throne and great authority.*

The Loch Ness Monster?

In Revelation, John describes a fearsome sort of beast.
You'll never see a creature like that at our local zoo —
A leopard with a lion's head and paws where feet should be instead.
I'd surely give a wide berth to that beast if I were you!

From the text, there is no question that the beast is clearly evil.
He casts a supersalesman's spell on all those who come near him.
From the dragon he's descended, and his evil is intended
To make all men forsake the Lord of Heaven and not fear Him.

If you should see a leopard with strange feet and lion's mane,
Don't turn and run, because if you've been saved, he won't attack.
Instead of going bonkers, you will be the one who conquers,
And the leopard will not have a chance to use you as a snack.

~ *Afterthought* ~

That beast is something like the ones invented by Walt Disney;
Isn't he?

Revelation 16:1, 18, 21

*¹Then I heard a loud voice from the temple telling the seven angels,
"Go and pour out on the earth the seven bowls of the wrath of God."*

*¹⁸. . . and a great earthquake
such as had never been since men were on the earth, . . .*

*²¹and great hailstones, heavy as a hundred-weight,
dropped on men from heaven, . . .*

The Seven Bowls of God's Wrath

In Revelation, God's wrath now unfolds
In the contents of seven large bowls,
    Seven plagues to exert
    A maximum hurt
Upon all unrepentant lost souls.

With the seventh bowl, lightning and thunder;
Great cities collapse, torn asunder.
    Then an earthquake exceeding
    Any Richter scale reading
Causes great Babylon to go under.

By now, the Lord's wrath, you'll have felt it,
And there's more — by great hailstones you're pelted.
    They're as big as your head.
    If one strikes you, you're dead.
But if the Lord hears your prayers, they'll have melted.

Revelation 16:12

[12]The sixth angel poured his bowl on the great river Euphrates, and its water dried up, . . .

He's Gonna Dry Up the Euphrates

If the Good Lord has the notion,
He can dry up any ocean.
He could cause such things to happen if He chose to.
In Revelation, no debate — He's
Gonna dry up the Euphrates.
That is what this chapter tells us He's supposed to.

In our lives, we must cross streams,
And that's not as easy as it seems.
If there's no bridge or ferryboat that's near you
When assistance you are needing,
You won't get that help by pleading
For the Lord to dry it up, 'cause he won't hear you.

So if you want to ford a river,
Don't sit on the bank and shiver,
Merely waiting for the Lord's help to get going,
And don't wait for help from elves —
God helps those who help themselves.
So just get yourself a rowboat and start rowing.

Revelation 17:3, 12

*³. . . and I saw a woman sitting on a scarlet beast
which was full of blasphemous names,
and it had seven heads and ten horns.*

*¹²". . . And the ten horns that you saw
are ten kings who have not yet received royal power, . . ."*

"Tin Horn" Kings

There's a beast with ten horns. That is weird.
Those horns were ten kings, it appeared,
    Foul deeds, their priority,
    Like Holmes' Moriarty —
And to conquer the world they were geared.

But Revelation's words seem to inform us
Those ten kings are not really enormous.
    Those ten horns, when they're tooted,
    Would sound tinny or muted —
They'd be just "tin horn" kings, who can't harm us.

Revelation 20:1-3

*¹Then I saw an angel coming down from heaven,
holding in his hand the key of the bottomless pit and a great chain.
²And he seized the dragon,
that ancient serpent, who is the Devil and Satan,
and bound him for a thousand years,
³and threw him into the pit, . . . till the thousand years were ended.
After that he must be loosed for a little while.*

He Got Out of the Pit Without a Bottom?

When Lucifer was tossed into the pit,
A pit without a bottom, we are told,
He dwelt down there for quite a bit — to wit,
For twelve months multiplied a thousand fold.

And when that one millennium had ended,
The devil was now free to roam the land.
Although it may be hard to comprehend it,
He was doing business back at the old stand.

Since he was in that pit and not repenting,
Just how Old Nick got out is still debated.
From the laws of physics, he'd still be descending
At a rate that must have been accelerated.

Old Nick was evil — fire and brimstone got him.
He was, without a doubt, a big-time meanie,
But his exit from that pit without a bottom
Would defy the talents of the great Houdini.

Revelation 6:2, 4–5, 8

²*And I saw, and behold, a white horse,
and its rider had a bow; and a crown was given to him,* . . .

⁴*And out came another horse, bright red;* . . .
⁵ . . . *and behold, a black horse,* . . .

⁸*And I saw, and behold, a pale horse,
and its rider's name was Death,* . . .

Revelation and the ERA

Here's a point I might add, parenthetical.
It's a small point, but it's catechetical.
    Nowadays, the Divinity
    Is without masculinity.
I'm old-fashioned — to me that's heretical.

Although God as an "It" seems bizarre,
With equal-rights zealots, that's par.
    Though it's hardly galactic,
    It's a devious tactic,
And it's carrying things a bit far.

In Revelation, four horsemen appear.
It has been that way year after year,
    But that same eschatology,
    In modern theology,
Would become "four horsepersons," I fear.

Are they, for Apocalypse, headed
As "equestriennes"? Never! I dread it.
    As they ride into battle,
    They'd be riding sidesaddle
If the equal rights people had said it.

Of the status quo, I'm a defender.
For me, the Lord's masculine gender.
    But when my wife looks askance,
    Do I alter my stance?
Do I hold fast — or do I surrender?

Postface

With your face wreathed in smiles at this fun with the Bible,
It would not be surprising, in fact, justifiable,
To reach the conclusion, though not verifiable,
That this book's perpetrator must be certifiable.

Biographical Note

Born in 1915 in St. Louis, Missouri, Ben Milder is the author of more than one thousand poems of light verse written over the past forty years. In 1979, his book *The Fine Art of Prescribing Glasses Without Making a Spectacle of Yourself* won the American Medical Writers Association's Best New Book of the Year Award (sometimes called the "Pulitzer Prize for medical texts"). Ben Milder's light verse has been published in many magazines and journals, including the *Palm Beach Post*, *Milwaukee Sentinel*, the *St. Louis Post-Dispatch*, *The Critic*, *Long Island Night Life*, *LIGHT Quarterly*, and the *Journal of Irreproducible Results*, and in the anthology *The Best of Medical Humor*. Professor Emeritus of Clinical Ophthalmology at Washington University School of Medicine, Dr. Milder resides in St. Louis with his wife, Jeanne.

Also available from **TIME BEING BOOKS**

EDWARD BOCCIA
No Matter How Good the Light Is: Poems by a Painter

LOUIS DANIEL BRODSKY
You Can't Go Back, Exactly
The Thorough Earth
Four and Twenty Blackbirds Soaring
Mississippi Vistas: Volume One of *A Mississippi Trilogy*
Falling from Heaven: Holocaust Poems of a Jew and a Gentile *(Brodsky and Heyen)*
Forever, for Now: Poems for a Later Love
Mistress Mississippi: Volume Three of *A Mississippi Trilogy*
A Gleam in the Eye: Poems for a First Baby
Gestapo Crows: Holocaust Poems
The Capital Café: Poems of Redneck, U.S.A.
Disappearing in Mississippi Latitudes: Volume Two of *A Mississippi Trilogy*
Paper-Whites for Lady Jane: Poems of a Midlife Love Affair
The Complete Poems of Louis Daniel Brodsky: Volume One, 1963–1967
Three Early Books of Poems by Louis Daniel Brodsky, 1967–1969: *The Easy Philosopher*, *"A Hard Coming of It" and Other Poems*, and *The Foul Rag-and-Bone Shop*
The Eleventh Lost Tribe: Poems of the Holocaust
Toward the Torah, Soaring: Poems of the Renascence of Faith
Yellow Bricks *(short fictions)*
Catchin' the Drift o' the Draft *(short fictions)*
This Here's a Merica *(short fictions)*

HARRY JAMES CARGAS (editor)
Telling the Tale: A Tribute to Elie Wiesel on the Occasion of His 65th Birthday — Essays, Reflections, and Poems

JUDITH CHALMER
Out of History's Junk Jar: Poems of a Mixed Inheritance

GERALD EARLY
How the War in the Streets Is Won: Poems on the Quest of Love and Faith

ALBERT GOLDBARTH
A Lineage of Ragpickers, Songpluckers, Elegiasts & Jewelers: Selected Poems of Jewish Family Life, 1973–1995

ROBERT HAMBLIN
From the Ground Up: Poems of One Southerner's Passage to Adulthood

WILLIAM HEYEN
Erika: Poems of the Holocaust
Falling from Heaven: Holocaust Poems of a Jew and a Gentile *(Brodsky and Heyen)*
Pterodactyl Rose: Poems of Ecology
Ribbons: The Gulf War — A Poem
The Host: Selected Poems, 1965–1990

TED HIRSCHFIELD
German Requiem: Poems of the War and the Atonement of a Third Reich Child

VIRGINIA V. JAMES HLAVSA
Waking October Leaves: Reanimations by a Small-Town Girl

RODGER KAMENETZ
The Missing Jew: New and Selected Poems
Stuck: Poems Midlife

NORBERT KRAPF
Somewhere in Southern Indiana: Poems of Midwestern Origins
Blue-Eyed Grass: Poems of Germany

ADRIAN C. LOUIS
Blood Thirsty Savages

LEO LUKE MARCELLO
Nothing Grows in One Place Forever: Poems of a Sicilian American

GARDNER McFALL
The Pilot's Daughter

JOSEPH MEREDITH
Hunter's Moon: Poems from Boyhood to Manhood

BEN MILDER
The Good Book Says . . . : Light Verse to Illuminate the Old Testament

JOSEPH STANTON
Imaginary Museum: Poems on Art

TIME BEING BOOKS
POETRY IN SIGHT AND SOUND

FOR OUR FREE CATALOG OR TO ORDER
(800) 331-6605 · FAX: (888) 301-9121 · http://www.timebeing.com